Praise for *Escaping the Build Trap*

"*Escaping the Build Trap* is, finally, the book that not only helps define product management, but puts it into organizational perspective. Melissa Perri does a masterful job of weaving together experience, examples, and expertise to paint a clear picture of the definition of product management (sorely missing from so many other books), the value it adds to a team and organization, and the commitment it takes to be good at it. This is a book for product managers but it's also a book for leaders. It's an indictment of the 'project' mindset and clear, practical manual for the product-led company. It's a must read."

—*Jeff Gothelf*, author of *Lean UX* and *Sense & Respond*

"A rare product management book that has the courage to suggest that when an entire company is product focused, the results can be astonishing."

—*Dave Pinke*, Practicing Law Institute

"Packed with actionable tools, techniques and real world case studies, *Escaping the Build Trap* offers executives, entrepreneurs and business leaders powerful insight as to how to create a product-centric organization to succeed in a world of accelerating innovation."

—*Barry O'Reilly*, founder of ExecCamp and author of *Unlearn* and *Lean Enterprise*

"Melissa's book is part of the new canon for product management. Too often product management is is seen as a bit of luck combined with a lot of ego. Melissa shows us its practice and discipline."

—*Jeff Patton*, product management coach and author of *User Story Mapping*

"*Escaping the Build Trap* is the missing guide that companies need to nail scaling their product organizations so they can effectively grow."

—*Shelley Perry*, venture partner at Insight Venture Partners

"If you're struggling to become a product-led organization, this needs to be on your bookshelf. From organizational culture to the product management role, Melissa has built a great guide to spotting and solving problems. I'm buying copies for my clients now."

—*Adrian Howard*, product coach at Quietstars

"There are many great books about product management, strategy, and development. I tend to recommend them with a footnote, such as, *Hey, this is startup focused, You'll need this other book, This covers the UX perspective,* or, *This is mostly for product owners in the context of Scrum. Escaping the Build Trap* is unique in that it is the complete package—no footnote needed. It's short and sweet, with a solid grounding in theory and actionable do-this-tomorrow tools. It gets to the meat of the matter—the shift from running a reactive feature or project factory to fostering a product-led, impact-focused organization. As a bonus, it is a fun read. The fictional Marquetly story holds it all together and is all too relatable if you've been doing this for a while. Hats off, Melissa! This rocks."

—*John Cutler*, product evangelist at Amplitude

"This is the sort of book you read and immediately want to share with everyone in your organization. It explains the importance of excellent product management in an organization, and offers practical approaches to help foster a culture of excellent product management. If you're in an organization that's shipping something, but you're not sure if you're shipping the right thing, stop right now, read the book, and share it."

—*Dave Zvenyach*, consultant and former director of 18F

Escaping the Build Trap

*How Effective Product Management
Creates Real Value*

Melissa Perri

Beijing · Boston · Farnham · Sebastopol · Tokyo

Escaping the Build Trap

by Melissa Perri

Published by O'Reilly Media, Inc., 1005 Gravenstein Highway North, Sebastopol, CA 95472.

O'Reilly books may be purchased for educational, business, or sales promotional use. Online editions are also available for most titles (*http://oreilly.com*). For more information, contact our corporate/institutional sales department: 800-998-9938 or *corporate@oreilly.com*.

Development Editor: Angela Rufino	**Interior Designer:** Monica Kamsvaag
Acquisitions Editor: Jessica Haberman	**Cover Designer:** Melissa Perri and
Production Editor: Justin Billing	Edie Freedman
Copyeditor: Octal Publishing, LLC	**Illustrator:** Rebecca Demarest and
Proofreader: Shannon Wright	Melissa Perri
Indexer: Judith McConville	

November 2018:   First Edition

Revision History for the First Edition

2018-11-01:   First Release
2019-02-22:   Second Release

See *http://oreilly.com/catalog/errata.csp?isbn=9781491973790* for release details.

978-1-491-97379-0

[LSI]

Contents

Preface

The point is, you can't keep doing the same thing and expect it to keep working. We had to do something different, but the really hard question was, "What is it?" We made plenty of mistakes along the way to answering that question, but the most important thing we identified was that we needed to know more about our customers and what problems they were really trying to solve in their businesses—even if they didn't neatly fit into an existing category of ours.

—MICHAEL DELL[1]

This book is for every product person. It's for the senior in college who wants to be a product manager but doesn't quite understand the full landscape of the job. It's for the first-time product manager who was thrown into the fray and is looking for guidance. It's for the product manager, just promoted to VP, who needs a guide to set up their organization so that it scales successfully. It's for the leaders of large organizations who are looking to obtain that competitive advantage.

About a decade ago, I was working as a product manager in an e-commerce company, chugging along, writing large requirement documents, shipping them to developers, and, frankly, thinking that I was the bomb. A much-needed dose of reality was thrown in my face when we began measuring the success of our products. I soon learned that my products were crap, and no one was using them.

That was my first realization that I was in what I now call, *the build trap*. I was so focused on shipping features and developing as many cool ideas (but mostly my own ideas) as I could that I didn't even think about the outcome of

---

1 TOM FOSTER, "MICHAEL DELL: HOW I BECAME AN ENTREPRENEUR AGAIN," INC. MAGAZINE, JULY - AUGUST 2014.

those features. I wasn't connecting the goals of my company or the needs of my users back to my work.

I wanted to get better. I wanted to create better products. At that time, the Lean Startup movement was taking shape and I learned about experimentation. An engineer by background, this spoke to me. "You mean I can test things in my work, just like science? I can use data to inform decisions? Sign me up," I thought.

I eagerly applied all the things I learned to my job as a product manager. I started seeing traction on my features. I began working with my team better. Together we became a lean, mean experimentation machine. And it worked: our products became better.

That experience inspired me. I wanted to learn more. I wanted more chances to implement these ways of working. I became a kid in a candy shop, soaking up every process and framework that would make me a better product manager.

A few years later, I began getting invited to share my experiences at conferences. I loved being able to talk about what I learned and how it helped me. I soon realized it was helping other people, too. More and more product managers, leaders, and designers came to me for advice. Eventually, in 2014, I became a consultant.

For the past few years, I have been brought in to teach product managers this systematic way of working. "Our product managers are stuck," the executives would tell me. "They need to learn how to talk to customers and think experimentally." The product managers I worked with were eager to learn, usually transferring in from another part of the company with no prior experience. They readily adopted the techniques, so excited to have a framework. I was thrilled. Helping people, seeing them get better, I found my calling—developing the future of product management.

I started writing *Escaping the Build Trap* two years ago for those very product managers. I wanted to help them become better.

But that evolved.

I never intended to take two years to write this book. It was supposed to be a three-month process. But, as I was nearing the end of my first draft, I was also checking back in with the product managers I had been teaching. A pattern had emerged. They had slipped back into old habits.

"Why are you not talking to users? Why did you stop experimenting?" I asked.

They cited a bunch of systemic problems.

"My bonus is tied to the features we ship. I need to get those out because it's getting close to the end of the year," I heard at one company.

"My manager was getting upset because we were not shipping. We were doing user research, but they couldn't see the value in it. I had to get something out the door or I'd get in trouble," said another.

I soon realized that it was not just the product managers that were stuck in the build trap, but the entire organization. Solving the processes for the team was not enough. It was about setting up the entire company to support good product management.

So I began rewriting this book to focus on the product-led organization. Then I was invited to lead a few large-scale product transformations at multibillion-dollar companies. I advised the C-Suite on becoming product-led, again eager to implement what I had learned. Little did I know how much I would learn through those experiences, in return.

The version of *Escaping the Build Trap* you are about to read is the fourth rewrite of this book in three years. It is a culmination of what I have learned about how roles, strategy, process, and organizational dynamics affect the value that a company can deliver.

This book is a guide to getting out of the build trap with great product management. We look at what it means to become and be a product-led organization (Figure P-1), which involves four key components:

- Creating a product manager role with the right responsibilities and structure
- Enabling those product managers with a strategy that promotes good decision making
- Understanding the process of determining what product to build, through experimentation and optimization
- Supporting everyone with the right organizational policies, culture, and rewards to allow product management to thrive

Figure P-1. *The product-led organization*

Throughout this book, you will read about a company called Marquetly. Although Marquetly is a fictitious company, its stories are based in reality, either from my own experiences as a full-time product manager or those of the companies I have worked with. You will follow Marquetly on its journey of escaping the build trap to become a product-led organization. If you want to see how your company measures up to being product-led, check out the last section of this book for a little quiz.

I've worn many hats in the past 10 years: product manager, UX designer, developer, CEO, entrepreneur, consultant, advisor, teacher, and student. The most important role to me has been that last one: student. The amount I've learned and continue to learn along the way, humbles me. I'm happy to share what I know in this book, but I know there's still much to learn.

I hope this book helps you find some guidance in an area that can sometimes feel overwhelming. I encourage you to keep learning. Keep experimenting. Keep getting better. Your customers are depending on you.

If you are interested in learning more about product management, check out our online school, Product Institute (*https://productinstitute.com*). We are continuously developing courses to help every product manager, from team member to executive. I am also excited to embark on a new partnership with Insight Venture Partners and Shelley Perry to develop the next generation of chief product officers at Produx Labs. The future is exciting for this field.

Thanks for reading,

Melissa Perri

CEO, Produx Labs

Acknowledgments

Writing this book was the most difficult undertaking of my career so far. It was a long, taxing journey that would not have been possible without the vast support of my family, friends, and colleagues. A lot of thanks are in order.

A special thank you to my team at Produx Labs and to my students at Product Institute. You are the reason I get up in the morning, knowing that we are building the future of product management together.

To Shelley Perry, of Insight Venture Partners, for your partnership, mentorship, and support. To Casey Cancellieri, for reviewing four versions of this book over the past two years, helping to shape where it is today.

To my publisher, O'Reilly, and editor, Angela Rufino. Your patience and guidance through this process has been exceptional.

To my editor Bridget Samburg for getting me to the finish line. I've learned so much about writing from you. This would not have been possible without your help.

I benefited from some very generous early—and last-minute—reviewers of this book. Thank you Giff Constable, Adrian Howard, Lane Goldstone, John Cutler, Simon Bennett, Dave Masters, Kate Gray, Blair Reeves, David Zvenyach, Ellen Chisa, Jeremy Horn, Ryan Harper, Dave Pinke, and Frances Close.

To those in the product management, UX design, Agile, Lean Startup, and Lean fields, from whom who I have learned so much in the past years, thank you for the in-depth conversations. Thank you for challenging my preconceived notions. Thank you for exposing me to other ways of working. Thank you for your support.

To my book club friends, who met with me every week for two years to swap ideas, provide feedback, and sometimes a much-needed venting space. To David Bland and Barry O'Reilly—I would never have finished this without you. Thank you for keeping me sane.

And, finally, I want to thank my family, because without them I would not be where I am today. They told a little girl it was possible to be like Bill Gates when she grew up. They encouraged her to wander around telling everyone that she would be a computer engineer one day. They still watch all her talks from conferences and cheer her on every step of the way.

Thank you to my parents, Joanne and Salvatore, and my sister, Jenny. You are my everything.

PART I

The Build Trap

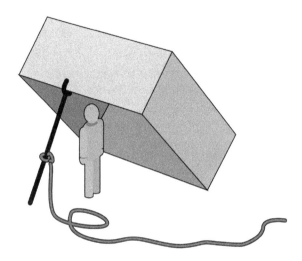

The build trap is when organizations become stuck measuring their success by outputs rather than outcomes. It's when they focus more on shipping and developing features rather than on the actual value those things produce. When companies stop producing real value for the users, they begin to lose market share, allowing them to be disrupted. Companies can get out of the build trap by setting themselves up to develop intentional and robust product management practices. At that point, product managers can find the opportunities to maximize business and customer value.

"Chris, your problem isn't just your product managers," I said. "They're definitely green, and you're going to have to hire some more senior people, but you have process, strategy, and organizational issues, as well, that are preventing you from hitting your goals."

The CEO of Marquetly, Chris, had called me to talk frankly about the state of Marquetly, an education company that provides online training for marketers. Experts in digital marketing, Marquetly professionals create classes through their online platform that any individual can take for a monthly subscription.

Six months earlier, Chris had hired me to train and coach the company's product managers. Marquetly was growing rapidly, with revenue growth year-over-year holding steady around 30%. The company hired hundreds of people in a very short amount of time, assigning them to all sorts of projects. Many of those people were developers, and they soon learned they needed product managers to work with them, after adopting an Agile framework called Scrum.

They moved marketing people, individuals with no prior experience in product management, into that role to work with the developers because they knew the audience for the school best. Marquetly's story was similar to those of other companies I had advised, and I knew that the issues were probably deeper than just skill based.

When I came into the company, I met with its VP of product, Karen. She had been hired three months earlier to oversee the dozens of new product managers.

"I am under a ridiculous amount of pressure," Karen told me. "The sales team has promised all of these features to enterprise clients. We've never serviced people in that market before, and now we have to build everything from scratch. I have 20 direct reports and a bunch of deadlines to hit. I have no time to be strategic at all."

The sales teams were frustrated, as well, and felt backed into a corner. "We need roadmaps, no one gives us anything to sell. This is how I make my money. I'm only out there promising things because the product teams aren't giving me anything," the head of sales told me.

The entire organization was at a standoff, with everyone pointing fingers at one another. All of them cited the lack of product management skills as the problem. "If only our product managers had deeper backlogs," the CTO lamented. "We would be set. We need them to start thinking of more solutions."

So I got to work with the product managers. I assessed their skills early on, watched them interact with their development and design teams, and gave them new frameworks to try. After about a month and a half, I had to break it to Chris that he needed to hire more experienced people if he wanted to succeed.

"Karen cannot be the only leader they are learning from here," I explained. "She has no time to mentor and coach dozens of people. If you want to grow the junior people, you will have to move some of these people back to the content division and hire real product managers."

"No, no, we can train them," he told me. "We can't hire a ton of new people. Just keep teaching them. Hire another coach if we need to."

I continued on with the training and brought in another coach to help. Many of the product managers were excited for the frameworks and the guidance. They readily adopted them, and, with some, we saw glimpses of early success in the way they approached problems and thought about their work. But that momentum was short lived.

When the teams did not have anything to ship by the third month, the leadership team became incensed. "They are not doing their jobs!" said the CEO. "We need to ship more features. Why are they not prioritizing better?" All fingers pointed back to bad product management. But that wasn't the actual problem.

The company was running in too many directions. At one point, there were 20 major projects in progress. When I say major, I really mean *major*. A new mobile app was being developed, along with a new backend system for the teachers to monitor their classes. These were large undertakings, meant for multiple teams, but only one product manager—and a junior one at that—and one development team were assigned to each.

They tried all they could to meet their deadlines, while practicing great product management techniques, but they were not set up for success. Deadlines had been set before I had come in. The different projects were committed to customers in their contracts. Whenever I suggested that we evaluate whether we should really be building a certain feature, there was a considerable amount of pushback from the product managers. "Leadership told me to do this. I have to ship this, or I won't get my bonus." They were handicapped by poor planning and poor strategy.

At the same time, Marquetly's revenue growth was declining, and the board was starting to pressure management. More mandates for features started trickling down to the teams. Karen tried all she could to push back, but the leaders were still insistent. "You don't understand. If we don't build these features, if we don't show the board we can ship, we will not be able to raise another round of funding," said the CEO.

Soon the product managers reverted to their old ways. They skipped the user research that they had been so steadily doing; it took time away from them writing up user stories for the development team. They all began focusing on getting as many features as possible out the door.

When the next release rolled around the following month, they had about 10 new features to put out to customers. The leadership team was ecstatic. "That's what I'm talking about! This is good product management," the CTO applauded them heartily at the review session. The next week, they shipped the features.

Then the calls began pouring in. The site was breaking because the features they rushed to launch were not well tested. Teachers were frustrated because there was so much new functionality that got in the way of them trying to accomplish their most important tasks: creating courses and responding to student comments. Many of the teachers decided to take their courses down, and the account managers were left scrambling to bring them back.

A few weeks later, we checked in on the adoption of the features on the student side. Nothing. No one was using them. All that work, all those features, and Marquetly was still in the same place. Its revenue growth was declining, and the company was feeling the heat.

The problem wasn't any single person or department's fault. The organization itself was not set up to succeed, which is what I was explaining to Chris during that meeting.

"I don't understand. How do other organizations succeed?" he asked. "How do they come back from this? What are we doing wrong?"

"It's not just about the skills of your product managers," I explained. "Some of them were doing well and adopting the right mindset. They were really trying to figure out how to deliver value, and had they been given the room to keep going that route, they would have succeeded. But you have so many organizational issues that are preventing them from succeeding."

"Like what?" he asked. "What can we improve?"

"Tell me, what is the most important thing you can achieve today?" I asked him.

"Revenue growth," he answered easily. "We need it to get back to thirty percent year over year at least."

"When I asked others in the company, they did not give me that answer," I told him. He looked a bit shocked. "Your CTO said the most important thing was the mobile strategy. When I asked why, he cited a board member. When I asked Karen what the most important thing was, she said acquiring more teachers on the teacher platform. When I asked the sales leader, he said getting more enterprise clients. No one is tying it back to your goal—the revenue. You are not aligned."

I continued. "A lot of it is due to having too many priorities. Everything is number one on your project list. You are peanut-buttering your strategy—meaning that you have so many strategic initiatives spread over very few people. You can't give one team a large objective and expect them to hit major goals in a month. Those things take time and manpower. You have to build up to them."

"But what about our product managers?" he asked. "Surely, they should be pushing back on this. So should my other leaders. If they don't think these are the right things to do, I want to hear it."

"Your company is not set up for that type of feedback. People are afraid to talk with you or their managers. You tie people's bonuses to shipping software, not to solving problems. They think they have to ship or they won't get paid," I said.

"Also, you have the wrong people in the product management role," I continued. "They don't know how to find the right solutions that will increase your revenue. They are marketers, not product managers. You need to build up a proper product management organization that can explore how to achieve value for the business. This is a specialized skill set."

Chris looked like he was at the end of his rope but pretty much ready for anything. "So what do I do? The company needs to succeed, Melissa. What can I do to fix this?"

"You're stuck in the build trap, Chris. To get out, you need to change the way you approach software development, both as a company and as a leader. You have to become product-led. That involves shifting the entire mentality of the organization from delivering to achieving outcomes. You will have to change your structure, your strategy, and not only the way you work but also the policies and rewards governing it."

He looked overwhelmed.

"Are you ready for this amount of change? It won't be easy, but it's 100% possible," I said.

"We can't keep going the way we are, or we'll go out of business," he said. "I'll do it." And so, we began.

Marquetly was a classic case of a company stuck in the build trap. The problem wasn't that it did not have a great idea or a great product but that the company itself was not set up to keep growing that product to succeed. The organization was missing the roles, strategy, process, and policies needed to really promote and sustain real value creation.

The build trap is a terrifying place for companies because it distracts them. Everyone is so focused on shipping more software that they lose sight of what is important: producing value for customers, hitting business goals, and innovating against competitors.

When we lose sight of what is important, when we forget what value means, the products we produce—and sometimes our companies themselves—fail. This has happened to organizations large and small.

Kodak failed to see digital photography disrupting it. Instead of responding to the change, it doubled down on how it always did things. When the company tried to innovate (which I talk about at the end of this book), it was not set up structurally to do so. It was too little, too late.

Microsoft, although not in danger of failing immediately, was on the path to disruption. It had been using the same strategic recipe over and over again, counting on Windows to carry its business, until CEO Satya Nadella came in. He realigned the company to a future strategy that would see it continue innovating and then adjusted the people working on those activities accordingly.

The build trap isn't just about shipping software. It's about realizing you have to change the way you've always done things. It's about confusing output-centric measures of progress with real measures of value. To get out of the build trap, you need look at the entire company, not just at the development team. Are you optimizing your organization to continually produce value? Are you set up to grow and sustain products as a company? This is what a product-led organization does.

In this book, I go into detail on how you can set up a product management organization to look for opportunities that maximize business and customer value. We start with the role of the product manager and how to create a structure that scales well. Then we dive into how strategy supports this role and how the product teams should work to achieve that strategy. And, finally, we talk about how the organization can set up its policies, culture, and reward systems to sustain this. Ultimately, this book provides you with a guide to get out of the build trap by becoming a product-led organization.

But first, let's go over how the build trap emerges and what signs you need to look out for. The first one is the misconception of value.

The Value Exchange System

Companies end up in the build trap when they misunderstand value. Instead of associating value with the outcomes they want to create for their businesses and customers, they measure value by the number of things they produce. Marquetly was a clear example of this when the leaders celebrated the 10 features the company shipped in a single month, but none of those features achieved their goals.

Let's go back to the basics to determine what true value is. Fundamentally, companies operate on a value exchange, as shown in Figure 1-1.

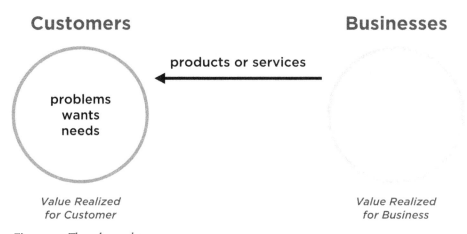

Figure 1-1. *The value exchange*

On one side, customers and users have problems, wants, and needs. On the other side are businesses that create products or services to resolve those problems and to fulfill those wants and needs. The customer realizes *value* only when these problems are resolved and these wants and needs are fulfilled. Then, and only then, do they provide value back to the business, as shown in Figure 1-2.

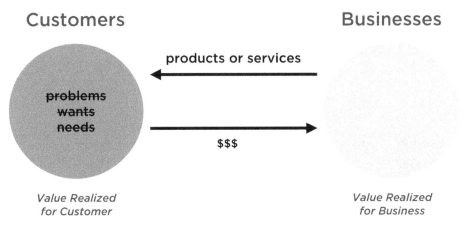

Figure 1-2. *The value exchange realized*

Value, from a business perspective, is pretty straightforward. It's something that can fuel your business: money, data, knowledge capital, or promotion. Every feature you build and any initiative you take as a company should result in some outcome that is tied back to that business value.

But value can be difficult to measure and to measure well from a customer or user perspective. Products and services are not inherently valuable. It's what they do for the customer or user that has the value—solving a problem, for example, or fulfilling a desire or need. Doing this repeatedly and reliably is what guides a company to success.

When companies do not understand their customers' or users' problems well, they cannot possibly define value for them. Instead of doing the work to learn this information about customers, they create a proxy that is easy to measure. "Value" becomes the quantity of features that are delivered, and, as a result, the number of features shipped becomes the primary metric of success.

These companies then motivate their employees and judge them for success with the same proxies. Developers are rewarded for writing tons of functional code. Designers are rewarded for fine-tuning interactions and creating pixel-perfect designs. Product managers are rewarded for writing long specification documents or, in an Agile world, creating extensive backlogs. The team is rewarded for shipping massive quantities of features. This way of thinking is detrimental yet pervasive.

I once worked with a company that made a data platform for enterprise companies. It had a total of 30 features, with about 40 more on the backlog, when I came in. When I measured the customer use of those existing features, we discovered people used only 2% of them consistently. And yet, development was underway to add more, instead of trying to reevaluate what they already had.

How did they end up there? A few reasons, and these apply to many companies stuck in the build trap. The company was playing a game of catch-up—trying to fast-follow its competitors on every feature it released. It didn't even know whether these features were working out well for their competitors, but management insisted on parity. This is the same trap Google+ fell into with Facebook—never differentiating enough, just copying.

The company also overpromised during the sales process, giving customers whatever it took to get the contract signed. The result was a ton of one-off features that satisfied the needs of only one client, rather than a strategic choice to build what would scale for many clients.

Instead of analyzing how each of these features provided unique value to its customers and moving the company strategy forward, the organization was stuck in reactive mode. It was not building with intent. And yet, it thought of itself as a successful company because it had a million features to talk about at user conferences. The company lost sight of what made its product attractive to customers—what made the company special.

You have to get to know your customers and users, deeply understanding their needs, to determine which products and services will fulfill needs both from the customer side and the business side. This is how you develop the Value Exchange System, as illustrated in Figure 1-3. To gain this understanding, companies need to get their employees closer to their customers and users so that they can learn from them, which means having the right policies throughout the organization to enable this.

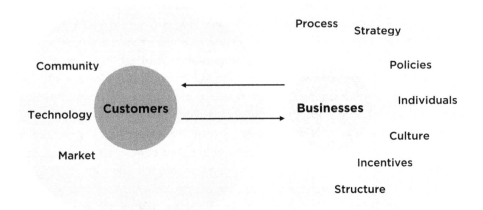

Figure 1-3. *The Value Exchange System*

Policies are one example of a constraint that affects this value exchange. This system is constrained by influences on both sides, as we saw in Figure 1-2.

Constraints on the Value Exchange System

Customers and users are influenced by the people they hang out with—their communities, families, and friends. They're also influenced by other technology —things available to them and on the market right now. Your customers and users don't exist in a vacuum, and so their wants and needs change according to what's around them. Likewise, your opportunities for how to address those wants and needs are constantly evolving. Directly controlling these surroundings is out of the hands of companies, so the only thing we can do is understand them better to know how to act.

Simultaneously, businesses face their own constraints. To realize the maximum value, organizations need to have the right individuals, the right processes, the right policies, the right strategy, and the right culture. Although many of the constraints and influences on the customer side are out of our control, businesses have full control over their own constraints and how they deal with them. When these constraints squeeze too tight, value is sacrificed on both sides of the system.

For example, many companies follow such a rigid development process and cadence that there is no opportunity to experiment. Whenever I start a new training or workshop, I say to product managers, "Raise your hand if you went back and iterated on the last thing you shipped." Normally, 15–20% of the people raise their hands. My next question is, "How do you know that what you shipped was successful?" The answers here usually revolve around meeting a deadline and finishing with bug-free code.

This is a prime example of a company that is optimized for outputs, instead of outcomes. *Outputs* are easily quantified things that we produce—number of products or features, number of releases, or velocity of development teams. *Outcomes* are the things that result when we finally deliver those features and the customer problems are solved. True value is realized in these outcomes, both for the business and for the user or customer.

Yet most companies I encounter are stuck in output mode, and their entire organization is optimized to increase the output. Their processes are driven by deadlines and by checking off as many features on a list as possible. Teams are rewarded and incentivized to build more. Policies exist for the purpose of pushing teams to write more code or ship more features, and efforts (like talking to customers) are seen as waste.

Most companies are unaware of the detrimental impact these factors have on their value production, and it's because they are not actually measuring the outcomes of their actions. They lose track of their strategy and vision, and they end up in the build trap.

To be strategic and to have people operate strategically, we need to stop judging teams based on the quantity of features shipped. We should instead define and measure value and then celebrate them for delivering on outcomes for our business and users. Then we should build products that help to achieve this.

Projects Versus Products Versus Services

Shifting into strategic thinking also requires a shift in the way we think about product development. Many companies operate on a project-based development cycle, in which they scope out work to be done, create deadlines and milestones, and then have the teams get to work. When the project is over, they move on to the next project. Many of these projects have their own measures of outcomes, but there is no aligning strategy above them.

There are many best-practice frameworks and certifications out there that promote project management–type thinking: PRojects IN Controlled Environments (PRINCE2), Project Management Institute, and Project Management Body of Knowledge (PMBOK). Companies stuck in the build trap usually confuse these frameworks for a product management framework.

To understand product management and how it differs from project management, we first need to define what a product is and why it is important.

Products, as I said before, are vehicles of value. They deliver value repeatedly to customers and users, without requiring the company to build something new every time. These can be hardware, software, consumer packaged goods, or any other artifacts in which human intervention is not needed to achieve value for the user. Microsoft Excel, baby food, Tinder, the iPhone—these are all products.

Services, unlike products, use human labor to primarily deliver value to the user. Service-based organizations are design agencies that create logos or brands for businesses, or they could be accounting companies where an accountant does your taxes. These services can be "productized," where they are the same service for the same price for every customer, but they still inherently need people to execute them. They can also be automated for scale, by creating a software product that executes on the service.

Many companies use a combination of products and services to deliver value. For example, many software companies that have an on-premises model, meaning they install the software directly on the computers of their users and have a services team go in and do the installation, customization, and setup. Any services or products that you need to be successful should be optimized together as a system to increase the flow of value to the user.

This is where projects come in. A *project* is a discrete scope of work that has a particular aim. It usually has a deadline, milestones, and specific outputs that will be delivered. When projects are complete, the aim is reached, and you move on to the next one. Projects are an essential part of product development, but the mentality of thinking only in projects will cause damage.

A product is something that needs to be nurtured and grown to maturity. This takes a long time. When you ship features to enhance a product, you are contributing to this overall success. This feature enhancement is a project, but your work may not be done when you are finished. You need to keep iterating by scoping out new projects to reach the overall outcome and be successful.

This is why the concept of product management—and that of having product managers—is so important for companies. You need the discipline to move toward organizing for products over projects. Companies that optimize their products to achieve value are called product-led organizations. These organizations are characterized by product-driven growth, scaling their organization through software products, and optimizing them until they reach the desired outcomes.

The Product-Led Organization

Product-led companies understand that the success of their products is the primary driver of growth and value for their company. They prioritize, organize, and strategize around product success. This is what gets them out of the build trap.

But, if you're not product-led, what are you? Many companies are, instead, led by sales, visionaries, or technology. All of these ways of organizing can land you in the build trap.

Sales-Led

Sales-led companies let their contracts define their product strategy. Remember my example of the data platform that had 30 features that no one used? That was a sales-led company. The product roadmap and direction were driven by what was promised to customers, without aligning back to the overall strategy.

Many small companies start off as sales-led, and that can be okay. As a startup, it's necessary to close that first big client and get the revenue needed to continue operating. So they'll go above and beyond for that client, working closely with them to define the product roadmap, taking all of their requests, and sometimes customizing things especially for them. But this way of working does not scale for long. When you have 50 to 100 customers or more, you cannot build everything uniquely to match the needs of each one, unless you want to be a bespoke agency. If that is not in the cards for you, you need to change your strategy to building features that apply to everyone, without customization.

Yet many companies that do not want to go the bespoke route operate as sales-led for far longer than they should. Their sales process gets ahead of their product strategy, and they continually need to play catch-up to make their commitments. This leaves no room for product teams to strategize or explore what could push the company further.

Visionary-Led

The easiest way to think of a *visionary-led* company is to consider Apple. Steve Jobs propelled that company forward, creating the product strategy, and got it over the hurdles of failed products to the success it is today. He pushed the boundaries of what was known, and the rest of the company followed.

Visionary-led companies can be very powerful—when you have the right visionary. But, there aren't too many Steve Jobses floating around. Also, when that visionary leaves, what happens to the product direction? It usually crumbles. This has been something Apple has had to contend with since CEO Tim Cook took over. The world is wondering what is next for Apple, after it has built up its existing products.

Operating as a visionary-led company is not sustainable. Innovation needs to be baked in to the system so that one person is not the weakest link. When you have 5,000 brains working on a problem (as opposed to one), you can harness that power better to succeed.

Technology-Led

Another common way of operating is the *technology-led* company. These companies are driven by the latest and coolest technology. The problem is that they often suffer from a lack of a market-facing, value-led strategy.

Technology is critical to a software company's success, but it cannot drive the product strategy. The product strategy must lead. Companies that let their technology lead the way often find themselves spinning their wheels, producing lots of very cool things, with no buyers.

Product strategy connects the business, market, and technology together so that they are all working in harmony. You need to be able to lead with a value proposition for your users, or you will not be able to make money.

Product-Led

This brings us back to being a *product-led* company. Product-led companies optimize for their business outcomes, align their product strategy to these goals, and then prioritize the most effective projects that will help develop those products into sustainable drivers of growth. To become product-led, you need to take a look at the roles, the strategy, the process, and the organization itself. This book helps you to do just that.

The good thing is that it's not technically difficult to make this change. You don't need to hire an entire new team. You don't need to scrap all your products and start over. What is needed, though, can sometimes be even more challenging to implement—and that's the mindset shift.

By implementing the tools in this book and practicing them consistently, you will begin to operate in a way that will shift your mentality there. But, ultimately, you need to stick with it. This will be challenging because it's a new way of thinking, for both individuals and companies. You need to begin focusing on outcomes and to adopt an experimental mindset to eliminate the uncertainty that what you are building will reach your goals.

5

What We Know and What We Don't

Product development is full of uncertainty. It's important to separate out the facts from the things that we need to learn. To do this, we explore the knowns and unknowns of our situation, as shown in Figure 5-1.

	Known	Unknown
Known	Facts	Questions
Unknown	Intuition	Discovery

Figure 5-1. *Knowns and unknowns*

When kicking off a project, it's best to begin by identifying what you know to be true about the situation—your *known knowns*. These are facts that you gather from data or critical requirements from customers. Now not all perceived requirements are necessary, but some of them are. These could be mandated by government regulations, or they could be basic needs that are required to do the job.

You need to separate these items out as facts and to label those that you are unsure about as our *known unknowns*. Known unknowns are clarified enough that you know which question to ask. They are assumptions that you want to test, data points that you can investigate, or problems that you can identify and explore. You use discovery methods and experimentation to clarify these, turn them into facts, and build to satisfy those facts.

Unknown knowns are those moments when you say, "I feel like this is the right thing to do." This is intuition from years of experience. Although we should all listen to our intuition, you should also be cautious because this is often where bias thrives. It's imperative to check and experiment to see whether your intuition is right.

The *unknown unknowns* are the things that you don't know you don't know. You don't know enough to ask the right questions or identify the knowledge gaps. These are the moments of surprise that need to be discovered. They happen when you are out talking to customers or you are analyzing seemingly unrelated data. They pop up during research. You need to be open to these discoveries and follow through on pursuing them because they could change the shape of your company.

Product management is the domain of recognizing and investigating the known unknowns and of reducing the universe around the unknown unknowns. Anyone can run with solutions based on known knowns. Those facts are readily available. But it takes a certain skill to be able to sift through the massive amounts of information and to identify the right questions to ask and when to ask them.

Product managers identify features and products that will solve customer problems while achieving business goals. They optimize the Value Exchange System.

Think of all of the different roles in a company, from sales and marketing to tech and design. So many of these functions don't cross over much between the tech side and business side. Product managers are the ones who fit right in the middle and translate needs into a product that will satisfy the customer while sustaining and growing the business.

Product managers are the key to becoming product-led. Yet so many companies put people without these capabilities into this role. Often they give them the wrong responsibilities or expectations, as well. Throughout Part II, we discuss what the role of the product manager is and how they can help you get out of the build trap.

The Role of the Product Manager

ROLE

STRATEGY

PROCESS

ORGANIZATION

Product management is a career, not just a role you play on a team. The product manager deeply understands both the business and the customer to identify the right opportunities to produce value. They are responsible for synthesizing multiple pieces of data, including user analytics, customer feedback, market research, and stakeholder opinions, and then determining in which direction the team should move. They keep the team focused on the why—why are we building this product, and what outcome will it produce? The chief product officer is the cornerstone of the product team in companies, helping to tie together the business outcomes to the roadmap and to represent its impact to the board. Companies need to create a standardized product management career path to attract the right talent and to provide them with growth opportunities in order to remain competitive in today's market.

It was my first month as a product manager, and I had just finished my first product specification document ever. I printed it for my boss to review and had been sitting there staring at it for five minutes through teary eyes, the way one looks at a beloved child. It had taken me a full week to prepare. Twenty-one pages long, it consisted of 14 beautifully designed mock-ups and every error case known to man. The developers were going to be so set. There would be no need to ask a single question. They would have everything they could possibly imagine in their hands to create the "change password" page for our site.

I did not even know what product management was until a few months earlier. At that first job, I learned that the role of the product manager was that of a creator and an arbitrator. We connected the development teams with the business, gathering requirements and translating them into features that people could actually use. I would frequently meet with the sales team to learn about what our customers were requesting. A few times, we interviewed actual customers to learn about their habits and needs. After I got my list of requirements, I would use Photoshop to figure out what the product would look like. It would be years before I learned that product management and UX design were not the same discipline.

After the designs were ready, I would begin writing the specification documents for engineers. I never actually knew what they did with them, but I learned that if I made them *really* detailed, the engineers wouldn't need to talk to me. According to most of my coworkers, that was considered a plus. So I would write up enormous documents—20- to 30-page product specifications detailing every single aspect of a given feature. The specifications included what would go into what that feature looked like and how it would function, all the way down to the minute details of what would happen when you push a button. Additionally, they covered scenarios, such as, what if there's an error state, or what if there's nothing entered in this form when you hit Submit? I was convinced that the more detailed I made the spec, the better I was at being a product manager.

When the spec document was done, it would be reviewed by my managers and shipped off to the developers. A few weeks or months later, I'd have a feature back to test. When I was sure everything was working correctly, we'd release to customers in the wee hours of the morning, when we could fix something without causing disruption if we botched it.

I was so proud when that "change password" page, my first product, birthed from a 21-page spec, was delivered to customers. My first real feature! Little did I know then that this whole release probably could have been accomplished in just a few conversations with good developers and about a tenth of the documentation or less. But that wasn't how I was taught product management. And that's not how most people are taught product management.

In this second part of the book, we talk about the role of the product manager, the path to learning product management, and how companies are commonly confused by the discipline. A great product manager must be able to interface with the business, technology, and design departments and to harness their collective knowledge. We look at these skills required to be a product manager and how to integrate this ever-crucial role into a company so that you can find the best solutions for your customers as well as your business.

6

Bad Product Manager Archetypes

There are few paths available today to learn product management. It isn't taught at college. Training programs on the job are usually lacking. Microsoft and Google are two of the only major companies that actually have an entry-level career path for product managers. Internships are few and far between. And most product managers you meet have made either a lateral move inside their company or have been "promoted" from software development.

If you are lucky enough to be taught product management, what you learn is usually very tactile: writing requirements documents (or user stories in Agile), planning meetings with developers, running check-in meetings, gathering requests from the business team, and testing for acceptance of the developed work and bugs. Many of these steps stem from the work of product managers who operate in a traditional Waterfall environment. This is the environment in which I learned.

Under a *Waterfall* process, the first step for a product manager is to talk to the people in the business—usually called *internal stakeholders*—and ask them for their input and requests. This is encouraged in the trainings of newly minted product managers: always satisfy your stakeholder. In my first role, I was told that the stakeholders were the marketing managers, my boss, and the sales teams. I met with them weekly, gained an understanding of what they needed accomplished, and then turned those requirements into specs.

After the requirements are detailed out, they are usually handed to the designers to create an attractive-looking interface, while working with the developers to ensure that the systems requirements are there. After the product managers approve the designers' work, the software engineers can begin coding.

Coding typically takes months, and, for large projects, it can even take years. Only at the very end of the process does the customer get to see the product.

Now, if you're sitting here wringing your hands, saying, "That's not how it should be done!" I'd agree with you. With the increased prominence of Agile methodologies, more and more people are seeing the flaws of a system that takes years to determine whether the given requirements are even the correct ones.

Many companies, such as our friends at Marquetly, have eagerly adopted Agile, thinking it was a silver bullet for creating more value in software, only to be disappointed. Why? Agile does indeed promote a better way of collaboration and a faster method of building software, but it largely ignores how to do effective product management.

Agile assumed that someone was doing that front-of-funnel part, generating and validating ideas, and instead optimized the production of software. Yet, that piece has been lost along the way, as companies believe that Agile is all you need to do successful software development. So, many product managers in Agile organizations still operate with this Waterfall mindset.

Being a great product manager takes a thorough understanding of your users, a careful analysis of your systems, and an ability to see and execute on opportunities for your market. When you go through the motions without active thinking, you end up with a lot of useless features. We rarely teach product managers how to think, and, even if we do, we don't measure this thinking for success. Instead, we are praised for writing detailed specifications or for making sure the developers are shipping on time.

When I ask people how they would define a product manager, I get lots of different answers—even from product managers themselves. "Product managers are the ones who come up with the ideas for what to build!" Or, "They are the voice of the customer!" And always, "A product manager is the CEO of the product!"

To understand what the product manager's role is not, you need to understand the common archetypes of bad product managers. Let's begin with that last one, given that I particularly hate it.

The Mini-CEO

Product managers are not the mini-CEOs of a product, yet 90% of the job postings I have seen for product managers describe them as being the mini-CEO. CEOs have sole authority over many things. They can fire people. They can change up teams. They can change directions. Product managers, on the other hand, can't change many of the things a CEO can in an organization. They especially don't have authority over people, because they are not people managers at the team level. Instead, they need to rely on influencing them to actually move in a certain direction.

Out of this wonderful CEO myth emerged an archetype of a very arrogant product manager who thinks they rule the world. I found one of these types at Marquetly. His name was Nick. Nick had just graduated from business school and was hired into the company as a product manager. All of the developers hated him. The UX designers, too. Why?

Frankly, Nick was terrible to the designers and developers. He specifically wanted to be a product manager because he fancied himself the next Steve Jobs, a visionary who would dictate, from on high, to his team everything they should build. Needless to say, the rest of his team didn't like that very much. He was frustrated. "The team won't listen to me. I can't get them to build what I want." Poor Nick. He just didn't understand his role.

I took him aside and said, "Look, I was once just like you, and let me tell you, this mindset does not work out in your favor. I came into OpenSky, our celebrity e-commerce site, grabbed on to that manager title, and didn't want to let go. I never wanted to hear criticism about my own ideas. After all, I was the visionary. This was my JOB. If anyone came to me with another idea, I dismissed it immediately. That attitude does not win you friends. And, honestly, I was miserable. My team didn't want to work with me."

I had his attention. I kept going. "So, one day, my boss took me aside and told me that if I didn't start winning over the team, I was going to fail. That's when I changed my approach. He reminded me that my job was to produce value, not develop my own ideas. It wasn't until I found some humility that I was able to create products that people loved. Before that, I was building things that did not produce the desired results for my customers, and no one adopted them. I also had an unmotivated team that was slow to deliver because they were not bought in."

Nick sat there and took it in. "I want to do well at this. Tell me what I have to do to get better and build cool products."

"Start listening to your team. Involve them. Listen to your customers and focus on their problems instead of your own solutions. Fall in love with those problems. Also, go seek out data to prove and validate your ideas. Turn to concrete evidence, rather than opinions." Nick took the advice to heart, and we worked on an approach together. He started with involving his team by holding a brainstorming session. Within a month, everyone's opinion of Nick began changing for the better. Then he made sure to follow up with them, ask their opinions, and give credit back to the team. He still had to win their trust back, but he was definitely going in the right direction.

Listening to everyone's opinions is important, but it doesn't mean a product manager should implement every suggestion. Swinging too far in that direction brings us to the other most common archetype of the product manager: the waiter.

The Waiter

The waiter is a product manager who, at heart, is an order taker. They go to their stakeholders, customers, or managers, ask for what they want, and turn those wants into a list of items to be developed. There is no goal. There is no vision. There is no decision making involved. This was the archetype of 90% of the product owner teams at Marquetly.

The most common question I get from product managers in this position is, "How do I prioritize?" Because they have no goal in which to provide context for trade-offs, it becomes a popularity contest for whomever is making the request. More often than not, the most important person gets their features prioritized. This happens frequently in very large companies. The product managers go out, with all the right intentions, to talk to their customers and learn what they want. But, instead of discovering problems, waiters ask, "What do you want?" The customer asks for a specific solution, and these product managers implement them. This is where you end up in what my friend David Bland, product advisor and consultant, calls the *product death cycle*, shown in Figure 6-1.

Figure 6-1. *The product death cycle, by David J. Bland (reprinted by permission of David J. Bland)*

The product death cycle is a specific form of the build trap. You are implementing ideas without validating them. It's not the customer's job to come up with their own solutions. That is your job. You need to deeply understand their problems and then determine the best solutions for them.

Waiters are reactive thinkers, not strategic thinkers. There's usually an amount of learned helplessness that contributes to that. They don't believe that they can push back on these solutions and dive deeper into problems. But that's not true. Customers want their problems solved. Leaders want to hit goals. Pushing back is essential to building a successful product. That's part of the job.

It's very possible to find the waiter archetype paired with another one, like project management. Because they are not focused on the *why*, they tend to focus a lot on the *when*. Project managers who are put into product management roles often become waiters waving a calendar.

The Former Project Manager

Product managers are not project managers, although a little project management is needed to execute on the role correctly. Project managers are responsible for the *when*. When will a project finish? Is everyone on track? Will we hit our deadline?

Product managers are responsible for the *why*? Why are we building this? How does it deliver value to our customers? How does it help meet the goals of the business? The latter questions are more difficult to answer than the former, and, too often, product managers who don't understand their roles well resort to doing that type of work. Many companies still think that the project manager and product manager are one and the same.

Agile methodologies distribute the responsibilities of the project manager across the team. These cross-functional teams have all the key players dedicated to ship a feature, so less coordination is needed across departments. Thus, project management is not needed as much as it once was when all of these people were in different areas of the business, splitting their time on different projects.

So, many of the project managers that once existed in these companies have now been made product managers or product owners. But they often lack the experience needed to be a great product manager. Answering *why* is very different than answering *when*. It requires a strategic mindset that understands the customer, business, market, and organization. This is a critical skill set for a great product manager.

7

A Great Product Manager

The real role of the product manager in the organization is to work with a team to create the right product that balances meeting business needs with solving user problems. To do that, they need to wear lots of different hats. An effective product manager must understand many sides of the company in order to do their job effectively. They need to understand the market and how the business works. They need to truly understand the vision and goal of the company. They also need deep empathy for the users for whom they are building products, to understand their needs.

The title "product manager" is misleading in itself. An effective product manager is not a manager. The position doesn't come with much direct authority. To be effective team leaders, product managers need to recognize team members' strengths and to work with them to achieve the common goal. They need to convince their team—and the rest of the company—that what they are working toward is the right thing to be building. These influencing skills are essential.

One of the biggest misconceptions about the role of a product manager is that they own the entire product and therefore can tell everyone what to build. Act this way, and you will only alienate the rest of your team. Product managers really own the "why" of what they are building. They know the goal at hand and understand which direction the team should be building toward, depending on company strategy. They communicate this direction to the rest of the team.

The product manager works with the rest of the team to develop the idea and then jumps in, as requirements become validated, to make sure that the product being created achieves the goals of the customer, user, and business. They then work to solidify the product vision, crafting it and communicating it, and then championing it. But, at the end of the day, it's the team, collectively, that really owns the product—the *what.*

Figuring out what to build takes a strategic and experimental approach. The product manager should be at the helm of these experiments, while continuing to identify and reveal every known unknown. At the beginning of product development, the known unknowns are usually around problem exploration and customer behavior, such as, "We're not sure what problem we are solving for the customer." As these unknowns begin to become clearer, the uncertainty then shifts to what will solve that customer problem.

Product managers connect the dots. They take input from customer research, expert information, market research, business direction, experiment results, and data analysis. Then they sift through and analyze that information, using it to create a product vision that will help to further the company and to solve the customers' needs.

To do that, a product manager must be humble enough in their approach to learn and take into account that they don't know all of the answers. They need to know that there are assumptions that they must tackle along the way, approaching them with a scientific mindset to validate them and to reduce risk. Ultimately, the goal for the product manager is that—reducing risk by focusing on learning. Most important, they need to know that not all good ideas are their own.

Tech Expert Versus Market Expert

A great product manager needs to be able to interface with the business, technology, and design departments and to harness their collective knowledge. One of the worst traits a product manager can have is the lone wolf mentality—the idea that they are the only one responsible for the success of their product. This causes them to become arrogant and dismissive of their teams' ideas. Great product managers understand that they will get further by taking advantage of the skills and expertise of their team.

Product managers do not come up with solutions in vacuums. They work with the UX designer to understand key workflows for the user, and experience factors could help reach the users' goals. They work with developers to determine how to launch a product or features quickly to the market.

A frequent question I get is, "What is the difference between UX design and product management?" These two disciplines overlap quite a bit, but user experience is only one piece of building a great product. Design is a critical component of a successful product, but, again, it's only one piece. Product management is about looking at the entire system—the requirements, the feature components, the value propositions, the user experience, the underlying business model, the pricing and the integrations—and figuring out how it can produce revenue for the company. It's about understanding the entire picture of the organization and figuring out how the product—not just the experience—fits into it.

One of the biggest mistakes companies make in hiring a product manager is trying to find either a technical or market expert. Product managers are not experts in either of these domains; they are experts in product management. That doesn't mean they don't need knowledge in either of these areas. They need to know just enough to talk with an engineer or a business person and to understand enough to make informed decisions.

A product manager must be tech literate, not tech fluent. That means they can discuss enough and understand enough about the technology to talk to developers and to make trade-off decisions. They know the right questions to ask engineers to understand the complexity of certain features or improvements. A product manager doesn't need to be able to code unless the product is highly technical and it's essential they understand the technology deeply to make decisions.

The same goes for the market. Although it's valuable for a product manager to know the market well, this is something they can learn. This is all about balancing the skill sets of your team. If you have highly-skilled market analysts, a great product manager knows how to talk to them, learn from them, and harness their skills.

This was a problem Marquetly fell into. They hired a few expert former marketers into the role of product manager, and, even though they really knew how to do marketing, they struggled with building products for an online education company. We ended up moving them over to the content side of the business, which made sense for both their career goals and the company's goals.

The product manager carefully balances the line between all disciplines to be able to strategize and decide what is best for the product. A great product manager listens intently to the inputs given from all their team members, but, at the end of the day, they make the difficult choices about what will be best for the business and the user.

A Great Product Manager

"So, what does a great product manager look like?" the team at Marquetly asked. I figured they were sick of listening to me opine, so I brought in Meghan, a product manager whom I knew. She worked on software for consumer mortgages at a large retail bank. She came to talk to the team about how she thinks of her role and what she does on a daily basis.

"I always start with our mortgage division's vision in mind," explained Meghan. "That's our business. The vision is to make it easier and more convenient for mortgage applicants to apply (or for mortgage holders to access), their information from anywhere."

Meghan was in charge of improving the experience for first-time mortgage applicants. She spent a lot of time talking to and learning from them. "I get really into empathizing with my users and figuring out what frustrates them. I call my customers Mary and Fred," she told the Marquetly team. "They live in New York City and are looking for their first home in Connecticut because Mary's pregnant and they want more space. You wouldn't believe the things they have to go through to apply for this mortgage. They have gone to their local bank branch multiple times in the past month to meet with a loan officer. They've filled out massive amounts of paperwork in the office, sometimes forgetting documents they needed, only to return the next day with them and do it all again. Then they've had to wait to see if they were qualified for the amount they needed." Meghan continued to explain the very detailed process the couple had to go through. It was clear she knew her customers well, and she knew their pain points.

But how did she decide which pain points to solve? Well, Meghan had already worked with her VP of product to identify the business goal that aligned with the vision of her department: to increase the amount of first-time applications that are submitted. At the time, 60% of first-time applicants who started the mortgage process did not finish with this bank and, instead, turned to competitors that handled the process with more grace.

Her goal was to improve that percentage. So, as she evaluated the customer needs and the problem points in their mortgage service offering, Meghan asked herself, "Will this help us increase the likelihood that these people will finish their application with us?"

The first thing Meghan wanted to understand was what was driving that 60% abandonment rate. She pulled the data to find out who had started the process but did not finish with their bank, and then she reached out to them. Quite a few of the people said they were frustrated with the process and eager for someone to make it better.

Meghan brought her team members, the developers and UX designer, to user research sessions periodically so that everyone could clearly understand the problems. Soon they found a pattern: many of the potential clients were asked to come to the office to verify documents, given that this could not be done online. Most of the people chose to go to another bank because it took too long to find an open appointment to come in for verification. Meghan followed up with a survey to a wider base and found that it was a prevalent issue—only 25% of the people who had this problem actually completed their applications with her bank.

Now that she had identified the problem, Meghan called the team together in a working session to generate ideas for a solution. They were careful not to jump to conclusions immediately, and they came up with several ways to solve the problem, while deciding to run a few short experiments to see which solution was the best.

Meghan explained to our team what one experiment entailed: manually taking on the work to understand how to establish an online system for uploading and verifying required documents for mortgages. The team worked with select first-time applicants and had them email the documents. The bank designated a person to review documents and to approve them during this experiment. Over that time, new applicants completed their applications 90% more often than those who had come into the office to have them verified.

By running the experiment, Meghan was able to prove the best way to reach their goal and increase the satisfaction of the users was by building out a way to have everything happen online. "We knew we couldn't start there, but that was our vision for the future. We had to work toward it, understanding more about each component along the way."

From there, Meghan's team worked backward, determining what could be in the first version of the new product, by prioritizing value and understanding effort. They decided to expand their successful experiment and to create more sustainable ways for users to send in their documentation while applying, but they still left the verification up to human beings. Although they were not able to verify everyone's information online, they were able to decrease the required verification visits by 50%. It was a great start.

They made plans to continue iterating on their solution, including putting in artificial intelligence (AI) components and online notaries, until they reached their goal of zero verification visits. "The biggest thing I've learned in product management is to always focus on the problem. If you anchor yourself with the *why*, you will be more likely to build the right thing," said Meghan.

Start with Why

Now, let's talk about what made Meghan and her team so successful. She began by asking Why?

- Why are we making everything digital in the mortgage space?
- Why even do this project?
- What's the desired result that we hope to achieve here?
- What does success look like?
- What happens if we make it all digital and nobody applies for mortgages?
- How are we mitigating that risk?

Too often, product managers dive into creating solutions without thinking through the associated risks. Each of the aforementioned questions represents a risk for Meghan that could potentially kill her project. Why do we do this? In many retail banks and other organizations, product managers are not given the opportunity to ask why. They are handed features and solutions from stakeholders or managers. Sometimes, these features are determined and committed during annual budgeting season. Other times, this is just seen as the manager's job —to dictate the solutions to build. When done this way, you invite the risk of failure, due to bias, in the execution of those solutions. All solution ideas are subject to bias, organizational or personal. The only way to fight this bias is to learn from users and to experiment.

In many cases when organizations hand down solutions, they skip setting success metrics and goals. Meghan's project could have gone very differently, if this was the case for her and had she simply been told, "Make the process of applying for a mortgage digital so that no one has to apply in person." Now what if she found that her customers did not want to apply online and were more comfortable doing so in the office? What if making the process digital caused the rate of completion to decline drastically? How could she have made decisions to correct those things, when she wasn't given the space to do so?

The biggest issue I hear from leaders, when I go in to help their organizations become product-led, is that their product managers won't step up and "own the product." But, this is a double-edged sword. In many cases, the product manager can do more to lead the product. They can question solutions and push back on things handed down. But the work required to gather data and prove the solution takes time. This is where people usually become confused between what Agile calls a *product owner* and a *product manager.*

When you look at the role of the product owner in most Scrum literature, the three responsibilities of the position include the following:

- Define the product backlog and create actionable user stories for the development teams.
- Groom and prioritize the work in the backlog.
- Accept the completed user stories to make sure the work fulfills the criteria.

These are the functions that are focused on and taught in the shorter product owner trainings, usually over a day or two. Although Scrum has a lot of information on the processes and rituals of what to do as a product owner, it leaves lots of questions unanswered and these questions are important for creating successful products:

- How do we determine value?
- How do we measure the success of our products in the market?
- How do we make sure we are building the right thing?
- How do we price and package our product?
- How do we bring our product to market?
- What makes sense to build versus buy?
- How can we integrate with third-party software to enter new markets?

Product ownership is just a piece of product management. A good product manager is taught how to prioritize work against clear, outcome-oriented goals, to define and discover real customer and business value, and to determine what processes are needed to reduce the uncertainty about the product's success in the market.

Without this background in product management, someone can effectively go through the motions of the product owner role in Scrum, but they can never be successful in making sure that they are building the right thing. In other words, product owner is a *role* you play on a Scrum team. Product manager is a *career.*

If you take your Scrum team away, and Scrum as a process, you are still a product manager. Product management and Scrum can work well together, but product management is not dependent on Scrum. This role should exist with any framework or process, and companies need to understand that in order to set their people up for success.

Most organizations do not give their people the necessary time to do product vision and research work. They would rather hold them responsible for a steady stream of outputs and measure success based on stacking backlogs and writing stories.

Meghan was successful in no small part because her manager and organization set her up for success. They worked together to define her goal, and her boss gave her space to go reach it. The company supported her in the work she needed to do to accomplish this. Most importantly, she had the advantage of being allowed to talk to her users.

By talking with the people who did not finish applying for their mortgage, she learned about the document verification problem. That's where she was able to say, "Aha! I believe, if I can find a way to verify these documents, we can get people to complete their mortgages." She found the problem to solve, rather than guessing at what needed to happen and then throwing solutions at problems that might or might not exist.

Meghan then worked with her team to figure out how to solve that problem. She was not a one-woman show. She involved the developers, the designers, the stakeholders, and anyone else needed to successfully execute. She involved people when she needed them. She did not take orders from stakeholders to create features without first diagnosing the problem. Instead, she leaned on stakeholders from the mortgage business to give her information and guidance as she crafted the right solution. She focused on the users and what they needed, rather than the wants of internal teams. After experimenting successfully, she was then able to rally the company around the vision for the entire feature.

Product managers ultimately play a few key roles, but one of the most important ones is being able to marry the business goals with the customer goals to achieve value. Good product managers are able to figure out how to achieve goals for the business by creating or optimizing products, all with a view toward solving actual customer problems. This is a very important skill set.

Too often, companies don't know what product managers are supposed to do or why they're important. I'm routinely told that people don't even think their company needs product managers. "The CEO comes up with everything." I hear that a lot. "We're not a big company, we are only a few hundred people, and the leadership team can handle it." The excuses pile up, and yet when I look at the companies who are making them, rarely are they successful in sustaining long-term value for their users. They are quickly disrupted, or, if they are larger, they slowly fizzle out. If you want to get out of the build trap and begin focusing on sustainable solutions and products that customers need and want, you must embrace product management.

One Role, Many Responsibilities

Chris was starting to get it. "Well, I really want product managers. What is the career path here? How do I keep them engaged and growing?" We talked through the responsibilities and how things change as you become more senior.

As a product manager, your roles and responsibilities will change depending on your context, the stage of your product, or your leadership position in the organization. Without a Scrum team or with a smaller team, you might be doing more strategy and validation work for a product that has not been defined yet. With a Scrum team, you might be more focused on the execution of solutions. As a manager of product managers, you might be leading strategy for a larger part of the product and coaching your teams to discover and execute well.

Scaled Agile Framework (SAFe) teaches this differently, and I think it's one of the weakest points in the entire framework. In SAFe, product managers are the managers of product owners and are responsible for external-facing interactions and work. They speak to the customers, they define the requirements and scope of the products to be built, and they communicate these down to the product owners. The product owners are internal facing, defining the components of the solution and working with developers to ship it.

I've trained dozens of teams who are using SAFe, and I have never seen it work well. Although the appeal of having a framework that lays out everything you need to do technology-wise in nice neat boxes sounds appealing, in practice it usually breaks down. The product owners are disconnected from their users and incapable of creating effective solutions because they do not understand the problems well. The product managers are essentially Waterfalling down the requirements, and the teams are not allowed to prove whether these are the right things to build. No one is doing validation work.

I have listened to many arguments that product owners do not have time to do both roles. In the current context, that's true. The product owners I speak with spend 40 hours a week writing tons of user stories. At that point, you need to ask, are those user stories even valuable? What are they prioritizing them against? How do they know that they will solve a problem? If you have one person spending that much time writing user stories, every week, you are most certainly in the build trap.

With a good strategy framework in place and ruthless prioritization around a few key goals, one person can effectively talk to customers, understand their problems, and help to define the solutions with the team. The amount of external versus internal work will shift, depending on the maturity and success of your product. But, you should never be doing all this work at once.

I teach my clients that product managers in senior roles (VPs, product leads, or middle managers) concentrate on defining the vision and strategy for the teams based on market research, an understanding of company goals and strategy, and by looking at the current state of success of their products. The product managers without Scrum teams or with smaller teams (a UX designer and one developer, for example) help validate and contribute to that strategy for future products. After we validate the direction, we create larger Scrum teams around these people and build out solutions.

It's important to have this flexibility in team size, as well, depending on the stage of your product. If you give a product manager a large Scrum team's backlog to maintain while you are in discovery mode, they will keep that backlog filled. But they will also be torn between keeping work flowing to the developers and trying to do the work to validate direction. As a result, neither ends up done well.

If you want to build products that create value for your businesses and customers, you need good product management foundations in your company. If you want a career path for your people, you need to give them this foundation so that they can grow into more senior roles. So remind your people to think like product managers. They might be playing the role of a product owner on a Scrum team most days, but you need them to think like a product manager in order to validate that you are building the right things.

8

The Product Manager Career Path

When organizations are small, their product teams are also small, which means that those people do literally everything. They span across many functions—and have to—in order to ensure the success of their company. As companies begin to scale, their product teams must scale, as well, and responsibilities become more defined. There are not enough hours in the day for one person to do all the work that is required to support a portfolio of products. This introduces more levels in the product management organization, and the responsibilities of these people change depending on the amount of tactical, strategic, and operational work they do.

Tactical work for a product manager focuses on the shorter-term actions of building features and getting them out the door. It includes the daily activities of breaking down and scoping out work with the developers and designers, in addition to crunching the data to determine what to do next.

Strategic work is about positioning the product and the company to win in the market and achieve goals. It looks at the future state of the product and the company and what it will take to get there.

Operational work is about tying the strategy back to the tactical work. Here is where product managers create a roadmap that connects the current state of the product to the future state and that aligns the teams around the work.

The foundations of working with a development team, diving into individual user needs and problems, and measuring data will always be relevant skills for a product manager at any level. Understanding the technical implications of building software or hardware, knowing how user experience can impact user value, and connecting that back to the business goals are basic building blocks of this discipline. But, as the portfolio or product scales, you need product people to start bringing this knowledge to a wider overview than just the features, to make sure everything is working together as a system. This is why the work starts to shift away from the tactical, as a product manager grows, as you can see in Figure 8-1.

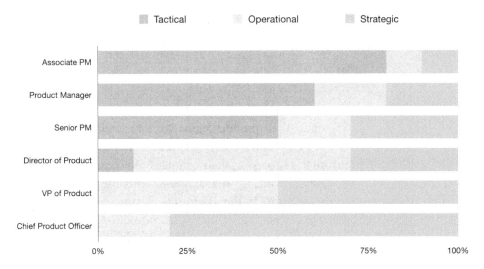

Figure 8-1. *Strategic, operational, and tactical percentages of product roles (for teams of over 10 people)*

Let's go over the typical product management career path:

- Associate product manager
- Product manager
- Senior product manager
- Director of product
- VP of product
- Chief product officer (CPO)

Associate Product Manager

The *associate product manager* role is the entry level position for a product manager. Yet, as I mentioned at the beginning of this part, there are not many of these roles available at companies besides Microsoft and Google. This is something we need to change in the industry. If companies want excellent product managers, they need to begin growing them.

Although I believe you can teach the foundations of product management to anyone with an affinity for the area and a willingness to learn, it's important to remember that this is a discipline that must be mastered *as a career*. As I've explained in this chapter, product management is not something you can learn in a two-day course, as so many Agile consultancies would like you to believe. You need to develop the skill set through experience and practice, just like any other specialty.

Developers learn their craft by pairing with senior architects and very experienced developers. A salesperson would learn the ropes from an experienced sales leader in their division. This is also what is needed for product management and is why it's important to have experienced people in product management who can pair with the junior people. Yet, as anyone who has ever tried to hire senior product people knows, there are not many out there on the market. The ones who are available are snapped up quickly. Why are we lacking so many people with experience in this role?

Setting up an associate product management or junior product management program is key. If you run a company or are in a position to craft your product organization, I encourage you to create this career option for people. Open up this role to people making the switch into product management, either straight out of school or from another career. Pair them with a senior product manager to teach them the ropes. Give them all the coaching they need. We create the senior people we need by giving junior people a chance.

Product Manager

The *product manager* works with a development team and UX designers to ideate and build the right solutions for the customers. They are the ones on the ground floor, talking to users, synthesizing the data, making the decisions from a feature perspective. Product managers are usually responsible for a feature or a set of features that are part of a larger packaged product.

It's a difficult role. The product manager needs to be strategic enough to help craft the vision of the features and how they fit into the overall product but tactical enough to ensure a smooth execution of the solution. They tend to skew more operational than strategic at this level because the responsibilities are around the shorter-term impact and delivery of features on the roadmap. Think of this as a quarterly focus.

The danger is when a product manager is 100% operational, focusing only on the process of shipping products and not on optimizing the feature from a holistic standpoint. When they only optimize for the day-to-day execution of the team, they usually fall behind in the strategy and visioning work that is needed for the success of the features. This is why it's imperative to push back as much project management effort as possible to the team and trust them to deliver.

Product managers are part of a larger product team, feeding data about the success of features to product people at the product and portfolio levels. This helps inform the strategy and direction of the product portfolio and organization. They report to a director of product or, at a smaller company, a VP of product.

A lot of companies have added a *product owner* title, which includes with the same responsibilities we discussed in the previous chapter on this topic. They see this as an entry-level role preceding that of product manager. As I explained earlier, when you think of a product manager as looking at only strategy and of a product owner only looking at tactical, you miss the connection between the vision and the day-to-day work. This gets you into the aforementioned danger of having the product person be too tactical. When you try to advance on the career ladder, the product owner will not have the experience with strategy that is needed to be effective. I believe it's best, as an industry, that we forgo product owner as a title and call everyone in this position a product manager so that there is a consistent and meaningful career path.

Senior Product Manager

A *senior product manager* is responsible for the same things as a product manager, but they oversee more scope or a more complex product. It is as high in the product management field as you can go as an individual contributor, meaning that they do not do people management. They want to concentrate on building products instead of growing a team. This is a particularly challenging role without direct reports because you do not have people to take over the operational side of the work. You must balance being highly strategic and highly operational.

This is the role for people who like difficult product problems. They want to work on new, innovative products and to chart new territory for the company. Their role is very similar to the architect role in development, which focuses more on laying the development structure and scaling it rather than managing other developers.

Senior product managers are critical to the success of companies of all sizes because they can operate more independently than many product managers. They are also usually entrepreneurial, which is a great trait, since these people are usually the ones who will start new product lines for businesses.

Director of Product

A *director of product* is usually found only at larger companies and is a critical role for scaling. At a certain point, a company will grow enough that there are too many people reporting into the head of product. This simultaneously happens as the scope of the products increases and the production of features ramps up. A director of product becomes necessary to help promote strategic alignment and operational efficiency, connecting their product group back to the product or portfolio vision.

The director of product is the first level of people management. They oversee a group of product managers who are aligned around a product in a portfolio or product line. The director of product is responsible for the strategic roadmap of the product, usually looking at a time horizon of a year. They are also responsible for the operational effectiveness of the team, making sure all product managers are aligned by the appropriate goals and working on the most important items to move the product forward.

VP of Product

Next is a *VP of product*. Someone in this role oversees the strategy and operations for an entire product line.

The VP of product is responsible for connecting the company goals back to the growth of their product line. With inputs from the people on their team and the data they provide, they set the vision and goals for the overall product. In large, enterprise companies, VPs of product are also directly responsible for the financial success of their product line, not just the delivery of product features. All the VPs of product in a large company must be aligned in their strategy and purpose, to ensure a successful portfolio of products.

A VP of product is usually the highest level in smaller companies because there is only one product and not multiple product lines. In these companies, the VPs of product are often responsible for a product team of one or just a few, and they have to dive into tactical aspects of product work to ensure that things get done. This means that these people tend to be more entrepreneurial and great at launching and growing new products.

In practice, VPs of product tend to skew either more strategic or more tactical. There are VPs who are great at being a product manager and at doing the work to grow a product themselves. Then there are VPs of product who focus more on the strategy and on figuring out growth plans for the product. A successful VP of product needs to fundamentally be more of a strategic person and to know that, in order to scale their organization, they need to hire in people who take over the tactical and operational components. This also allows them to grow into the role of CPO, which is primarily strategic.

Chief Product Officer

The CPO is a fairly new yet critical role for organizations. A CPO oversees a company's entire product portfolio. This is the highest role of a product manager, and it represents a seat at the executive table of a company.

A company should think about adding a CPO when it starts to develop its second product, expands into another geography, or merges with another company. This role is critical to ensure that the entire portfolio is working together to achieve the company goals.

The CPO is responsible for driving the economic success of the business through the growth of the product portfolio. Although a VP of product needs to understand how their product roadmap affects the economics of the company, a CPO needs to do that across all products. They work with the VPs of product to ensure that every product is strategically aligned to the company's objectives and that each product has what it needs, from a resource and people perspective, to reach the established goals.

A CPO needs to be able to interface at the board level, as well. Shelley Perry, a venture partner for Insight Venture Partners and an expert on the role of the CPOs, explains it as follows: "Board members care about the financial impacts of the technology and product decisions. A successful CPO needs to be able to translate their actions into terms the board will understand."

Perry helps find the best CPOs for Insight's portfolio companies, which are all growth-stage software companies. She has a few key personality traits that she looks for when hiring a CPO:

> Assuming they are already skilled in all aspects of product, technology, and financial management, those that make the best chief product officers also have three key traits that set them apart: they inspire confidence, empathize, and are relentless and resilient.

To inspire confidence in the product direction, CPOs work across many functions to gain buy in and alignment. It's necessary that they bridge and unify the key departments and stakeholders. They do this by adjusting the way they tell a story and by conducting themselves among groups in an authentic way. This trait also enables them to get things through influence versus direct authority.

As with other C-Suite roles, CPOs are rarely in a position to make decisions solely based on the textbook principles of product management. Other factors, like current state, financial objective, and rate of organizational change, must come into play. By empathizing with the other members of their peer group, their customers, and their teams, CPOs can find a way forward that aligns all the goals. This allows them to also traverse adjacent industries and to immerse themselves in the customer perspective.

Finally, a CPO must be relentless and resilient. They need the desire to dig in and find out what is working and what is not. They are constantly assessing and analyzing, trying to prove their hypotheses right or wrong, and holding themselves accountable to data. When something does not work as planned, they need the tenacity to keep digging and find out what will.

Having a strong product leader in the C-Suite is a critical step to becoming product-led. Unfortunately, there are not many CPOs available on the market at the moment, because this field is still emerging. My company, Produx Labs, has partnered with Insight Venture Partners to create a CPO Accelerator that develops VPs of product into CPOs for their companies. We're excited to be developing the future leaders of growth-stage companies that can help create great product-led organizations.

9

Organizing Your Teams

The way you structure your product teams and organize them around the work that needs to be done on features and products is incredibly important for the success of your product development. Companies tend to organize in three main ways: value streams, features, and technical components.

When I came in, Marquetly was structured around technical components. "Our Agile coach suggested we put Scrum teams over every area of our product so we have coverage," said the CTO. Although this makes sense in theory, in practice it helped to promote poor product management.

During a workshop for the product team on good product management skills, I was stressing the importance of solid foundations, when one of the product owners chimed in. "Most of this is really great. I'd like to work this way, but I can't because I have to keep the backlogs full for our login API. If I don't do that, my developers won't have anything to do."

"Is it a new API?" I asked. "Are there massive issues with it right now that you're trying to fix?" Turns out there were no major problems with it. It had been working fine. "What's your goal? When do you know that your API is done and that you can move on to something else?"

"Oh, no, no, no," she said. "This is what I own. This API is what our team owns, and we'll never get something different. This is our feature—we just own this forever."

They were actively working on a technical component that was already in a steady state, where it was optimized and functional. This did not need to be worked on to achieve the company goals, and yet here she was creating work for her team because she had been told it was what she owned and could work on.

A similar issue happens when teams are organized around specific features. A lot of teams do this to get *coverage*—ownership over every part of the product. Although this is good if you are literally starting from scratch and do not have a product organization set up, but, over time, it promotes a very output-oriented mindset. Instead of working toward a goal and saying no to anything that doesn't get us there, we tend to look for ways to develop more things related to our little slice of the product.

If we take a step back and align the work of these teams to the overall vision of the product and strategy (which we talk about in the next section), we find that much of that work really shouldn't have been prioritized. When features are stable, we should monitor them but then move on to the more important work needed to support our strategy.

But, you might be asking: don't you want teams to own all features so that you have a way to make sure someone is looking after them? Yes and no. To organize teams effectively, you need to balance the coverage and scope of teams with the goals you are trying to achieve.

When companies are small, you can organize effectively around goals you are trying to reach. Consider how TransferWise does it. This London-based company does electronic transfers. You can send money to different countries in other currencies with very low fees, compared to what the banks charge. TransferWise has a relatively small number of product teams at around 12. The way they organize their teams—around strategic goals—allows them to stay small and still get an immense amount of work done.

One team is focused on retention, another on implementing new currencies, and another on acquiring new users. Each of the teams has ownership of their goal and is judged for success based on their outcomes. They are also allowed to work across all products to do whatever is needed to reach those goals. It takes a huge amount of coordination across the product teams, so everyone is responsible for collaborating intensely with one another. Even though the coordination might seem like a handful, having fewer teams makes them ruthlessly prioritize around the most important initiatives. There's no useless work.

This structure also creates a nice redundancy throughout the company, so that important information about a single product is not stuck in the head of one person. If someone leaves, they don't need to worry about all that ingrained knowledge going with them. If one team is busy with work, another team doesn't need to wait for them to fix a bug because they own that piece of the product and no one else knows how to fix it.

TransferWise is an extreme example, but it works well for them. As companies scale, and especially as they begin to maintain more than one product, this approach might not be a viable option. We have to add in another component to organizing teams, but we still want to keep the product strategy and the goal-oriented nature. In addition to these things, we also look at the value streams of the organization.

A *value stream* is all of the activities needed to deliver value to the customer. That includes the processes, from discovering the problem, setting the goals, and conceiving of the idea, to delivering the actual product or service. Every organization should strive to optimize this flow in order to get value out the door faster to customers. To do that, it makes sense to organize your teams around the value stream.

How do you organize this way? First you begin with the customer or user—whomever is consuming your product at the end of the day. What is the value that you are providing them? Then work backward. What are the touchpoints they have with your company on the way to receiving that value? Having identified these, how do you organize to optimize and streamline that journey for them? How do you optimize to provide more value, faster?

Many companies are confused by the word *product*. You say product and people think of an app, a feature, or an interface. If you think back to our diagram on the value exchange in Figure 1-1, products are vehicles for value. So, if your app, interface, or feature is not inherently adding value on its own, it's just a piece of the entire product. That doesn't mean no one needs to manage it. It just means you have to look beyond just that piece to understand how to manage for value delivery and creation.

Consider an insurance company. The products for an insurance company are what they sell to customers: car insurance, home insurance, life insurance, and so on. I buy car insurance because it provides me with peace of mind in case I get into an accident—that's value. Having an iPhone app that allows you to manage your car insurance, for example, is only a piece of that product's value stream. That app can help get me more information on my insurance policy or find options if I get in an accident. This functionality is valuable to me, but the app on its own is not enough value. I still need the car insurance product.

You can still have a product manager owning that iPhone app's experience, but you must make sure that they are part of the larger division that holds the true value—the car insurance division. This structure makes it possible to set strategy at the division level, with the product manager able to execute on product initiatives that tie to their product. Keeping the strategy and the value execution together is key. This approach allows you to really evaluate the work happening on your teams and to make sure it's essential to achieving your strategy.

As your company scales to include more products, you will need more levels of management to effectively oversee the various areas. However, you don't want to overdo it. Having the right number of levels also has a large impact on your strategy (which we'll talk about in the next section). By minimizing the number of layers and by giving product managers more scope over their product areas, you can effectively create a product organization with a structure that supports the product strategy.

Marquetly's Product Team

The product team at Marquetly was not designed to scale. The company had 20 product teams organized around components, with its product managers writing those user stories every second of every day. Most of the 20 product managers should have been considered associate product managers because they were new to the role. They also had only one senior person, Karen, the VP, to coach them.

"How should we build out this organization?" Chris asked me one day.

"We need to restructure around value streams, but first you need more senior people, and you should start by hiring an experienced chief product officer," I explained. "Karen is a fantastic VP of product, but she can't operate at the level of a chief product officer. Although she is very good at the tactical and strategic work of determining a single product vision and growing it, she doesn't understand how to manage a portfolio of products. She can't interface with the board and explain to them how they will grow this business from a revenue standpoint. She's also overwhelmed and still eager to learn. Karen can run the product team and set the vision for your current teacher platform, but she needs someone to help with the strategic and organizational decisions, as well as coach her into that next level."

There was more: "In the meantime, you also need more senior people, and you need to restructure your teams. You have everyone spread around components of features, but there is no one pulling together a holistic vision for each value stream. For example, you want to grow the teacher platform such that they can upload their videos and create courses. Right now, you have four different product managers working on it, but no one is responsible for the overall vision. There is no driving consensus on what that platform will be. Karen has a strong vision for the teacher experience, but she can't manage both the student experience and that at the same time. I would find another VP of product to take over the student experience."

Figure 9-1 depicts a first pass of the desired end state of the product organization for Marquetly. We started with this knowing what our product was today, but we wanted to iterate as a stronger product vision emerged after a CPO was hired. You can't build an organizational structure without a product vision, because the value streams are not apparent. Luckily, Marquetly had enough of a vision to make a considerable impact in the short term.

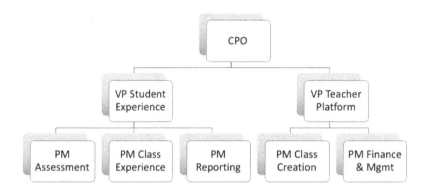

Figure 9-1. *Final state Marquetly product management organizational chart*

Here, we were balancing the senior and junior folks and making sure we could scale appropriately. You may notice that there are not 20 people in the organization. Why? When we began breaking the product into value streams and organizing around feature sets that delivered whole value (instead of component areas, like an API), we found that there were not 20 areas. This often happens when teams restructure around value instead of components. They find they do not need as many people to accomplish their goals.

Pandora, a subscription music service, is an example of a company that found the constraint of having a small team actually an opportunity for success. They were able to scale to 70 million monthly users with just 40 engineers,[1] by ruthlessly prioritizing the work the company was doing on a quarterly basis. This

---

1 "This Product Prioritization System Nabbed Pandora 70 Million Monthly Users with Just 40 Engineers", First Round. *http://bit.ly/2O4KmR2.*

laid the groundwork for Pandora's $7 billion valuation today. Staying small forced it to focus on getting the most important work done to grow the business.

Product managers need room to manage toward an entire outcome-oriented goal. This means that people need to be aligned around value and to have the scope to actually make measurable impact toward it. This gets to what we were talking about earlier—organizing teams around your strategy, which is the most important work for your business.

When organizations lack a coherent product strategy that is ruthlessly prioritized around a few key goals, they end up spreading themselves thin. There are many teams working to optimize components but not the whole. Don't forget that, to make a considerable impact, you need to have everyone going in the same direction, working toward the same goals, the way Pandora did. In the next part, we talk about how to create a strategy that ensures you are doing this.

PART III

Strategy

A good strategy is not a plan; it's a framework that helps you make decisions. Product strategy connects the vision and economic outcomes of the company back to product portfolio, individual product initiatives, and solution options for the teams. Strategy creation is the process of determining the direction of the company and developing the framework in which people make decisions. Strategies are created at each level and then deployed across the organization.

In 2005, Netflix had more than four million subscribers and 50,000 movie and TV show titles in its DVD catalog, which represented significant growth in the six years it had been around. The entire company had rallied around the vision its founder had set, after he had been embarrassed by a $20 late fee at Blockbuster: "To provide movies and TV shows in the most convenient and easy way for customers." With its customer-focused vision, Netflix set out to completely disrupt the way the market consumed entertainment.

At the time, the company was heavily invested in the DVD space, where it had been incredibly successful. But it didn't see DVDs as the end point. In an interview in 2005 with *Inc.* magazine, Founder and CEO Reed Hastings said this:

> *DVDs will continue to generate big profits in the near future. Netflix has at least another decade of dominance ahead of it. But movies over the Internet are coming, and at some point it will become big business. We started investing 1% to 2% of revenue every year in downloading, and I think it's tremendously exciting because it will fundamentally lower our mailing costs. We want to be ready when video-on-demand happens. That's why the company is called Netflix, not DVD-by-Mail.[1]*

Netflix knew that, if it truly wanted to become the most convenient vehicle by which people would watch movies, it had to figure out a way to get entertainment into the hands of its users faster. Even though the internet was rapidly developing in the early 2000s, streaming was not a viable option. It took an entire night for me to download just a simple audio album from Napster in those days. A DVD would be 1,000 times larger than one of those files. But, by 2005, the internet was getting to a point where this could actually be possible. This development helped inform the company's overall strategy for the future:[2]

1. Get big on DVD

2. Lead streaming

3. Expand worldwide

---

1 Reed Hastings, as told to Patrick J. Sauer, "How I Did It: Reed Hastings, Netflix," *Inc.* magazine, December 1, 2005. *http://bit.ly/2ONZO9n*.

2 Gibson Biddle, "How to Run a Quarterly Product Strategy Meeting: A Board Meeting for Product," Medium, June 21, 2017. *http://bit.ly/2z4Y4h7*.

Because Netflix was already dabbling in the online video-on-demand space, the company was able to determine that people were interested. As the internet became faster, the company expected to see more people downloading videos on demand rather than receiving DVDs by mail. It made sense from a strategy standpoint—instant entertainment is definitely convenient. And yet, not as many people were adopting this offering as they had hoped. Why?

Stepping back and looking at the situation from the customer's point of view, Netflix realized that the only internet-enabled devices at the time were laptops and home computers. That wasn't the most convenient or delightful way to watch movies all of the time. Occasionally, yes, but it wasn't the preferred way to constantly consume entertainment. Most people would rather watch them on a big screen with family and friends. This was a problem the company decided to tackle in order to lead the streaming market. It decided to create a way for subscribes to watch content on any device.

So, Netflix decided to build its own internet-connected device that plugged into TVs. They called it Project Griffin.[3] The company spent years developing the product, testing and validating the device. Everyone was amped. Then, a few days before launch in 2007, Reed Hastings sent out an email to the entire company saying to stop production on it. "Just kill it", he said.

All that time, all that money, wiped out, a few days before launch. Why?

Hastings realized that if he launched a hardware device, he could not partner with anyone else. He would be in the business of hardware, not software or entertainment. That wasn't part of the Netflix core vision. So, he made the hard call and decided to stop a project, even when it was so close to being done, because it did not align with the overall strategy.

Instead, Netflix spun off Project Griffin as a separate company, which you know today as Roku. Then it turned its sights to finding a partner with a device for which they could build an app. They approached Microsoft, and, six months later, Netflix was enabled on more than one million Xbox devices, accomplishing the goal of gaining more streaming customers.

The Netflix story is the epitome of excellent strategy, and we're lucky that they've talked openly about it so that we can learn from it. Yet, even with this strategy framework, the company still got caught in the build trap with Project

---

3 Austin Carr, "Inside Netflix's Project Griffin: The Forgotten History Of Roku Under Reed Hastings," Fast Company. http://bit.ly/2Pnm2yA.

Griffin and Roku. Why? It's easy to become distracted, as Hastings explained in an interview with *The New York Times*:[4]

> After we eventually won the Blockbuster battle, I looked back and realized all those things distracted us. They didn't help, and they marginally hurt. The reason we won is because we improved our everyday service of shipping and delivering. That experience grounded us. Executing better on the core mission is the way to win.

Luckily, the company realized this sooner rather than later, and, by turning back to its strategic framework and core mission to make people happy, it was able to get out of the build trap and remain out. This has made Netflix one of the most successful software companies to date. How did Netflix do it?

First, it focused the entire company around a solid vision. This vision has evolved over time as the market has evolved. Now the vision for Netflix is, "Becoming the best global entertainment distribution service, licensing entertainment content around the world, creating markets that are accessible to film makers, and helping content creators around the world to find a global audience." This vision states not only why the company exists but also the plan for getting there. It aligns the team in the right direction.

Netflix then self-organized around key outcomes and strategies to help reach its goals. Gibson Biddle, who was a VP of product at Netflix from 2005 to 2010, talks about aligning his team around a common guideline for evaluating its product strategy. That guideline was to "delight customers, in margin-enhancing, hard-to-copy ways." He set goals that would accomplish this and would help Netflix execute on the company vision around key initiatives (Table III-1), including personalization, instant access to entertainment, and ease of use. Teams were then able to explore tactics to accomplish these goals, and they were held accountable to success metrics for each.

---

4 James B. Stewart, " Netflix Looks Back on Its Near-Death Spiral," The New York Times, April 26, 2013. *https://nyti.ms/2JgiRmF.*

Table III-1. *Gibson Biddle, Netflix strategy, 2007*

Key strategies	Tactics	Metrics
Personalized	Ratings Wizard, Netflix Prize	Percentage of customers who rate ≥ 50 titles at 6 weeks; RMSE
Instant	Hub expansion, streaming	Percentage of disks delivered in one day; percentage of customers who watch ≥ 15 min/month
Margin-enhancing	Previously viewed, advertising, price & plan testing	Gross margin, LTV
Easy	Simplify and kill; progressive disclosure	Percentage of customers with ≥ 3 titles in queue on day one

This combination of vision, goals, and key initiatives helps create a system in which Netflix can make decisions about its products—sometimes difficult decisions, like killing Roku. Netflix can change tactics or kill ideas because it commits itself not to the solutions they are building but rather to the outcomes these solutions produce. The company then enforces this mentality with a product strategy that is coherently aligned and decision enabling.

The powerful thing about a strategic framework like the one Netflix uses is that it forces you to think about the whole before zooming in on the details. When we're developing software, we often think of the details and neglect the big picture. What feature can we build? How do we optimize that feature? When will it be delivered? When a company thinks only about the feature-level model, it loses track of the outcomes those features should produce. That is what lands you in the build trap.

In Chapter 10, I cover the building blocks of strategy, starting from the big picture of the company vision and then continuing down through the company to the activities of the teams. We talk about how good strategy focuses and aligns the product teams around achieving the right outcomes.

10

What Is Strategy?

It was a Monday afternoon, and one of the teams I was coaching at Marquetly was gathered around a table in a conference room, planning its next experiment. It had been exploring how to increase user acquisition of its product, but there was a problem. Team members were not sure what was preventing people from signing up. This meeting was to figure out what was getting in the way.

"We have the sign-up funnel, and we can see that people are falling off on Step 3. We need to start diagnosing exactly *why* they are falling off. That's our goal for this week. How do we make that happen?" I asked the team, just as the CTO wandered into our meeting and took a seat.

"We have to figure out a way to get in touch with these people," one of our developers said. "Maybe we can try to reach out—"

He was abruptly cut off by the CTO. "I do not understand what your product strategy is. What is it?"

"I'm not sure what you mean," I replied. "They're trying to diagnose the problem so they can decide what they should build later. They have a goal, but they're discovering the problems surrounding it."

"No," he said. "You need to have a strategy. By the end of a week, I want to see a specification document that has all the content for the site laid out, the backend you want, and everything you are going to build over the next three months."

I pushed back. "How can they possibly tell you what they should build if they're not sure why they are building it? They can't figure out the right product until they know what problem they are solving."

The CTO didn't want a strategy. He wanted a plan.

Good strategy isn't a detailed plan. It's a framework that helps you make decisions. Too often, people think of their product strategy as a document made up of a stakeholder's wish list of features and detailed information on how those wishes should be accomplished. And they're peppered with a ton of buzzwords like *platform* or *innovation*.

Communicating the end state of a product is not inherently wrong. You should be striving toward a vision. However, it becomes dangerous when we commit to these visions and lofty feature sets without validation. When I ask people what their strategy is and they begin reciting their to-do's, I always ask this follow-up question: "How do you know that *this* is the right thing to build?" Most of the time, I cannot get a straight answer to that question, or I hear, "I have no idea, but my boss told me to build it."

Not being one to stop there, I go up a level and ask why the team is building this product. The answers, at this point, become really interesting. They cite market research or the need to have feature parity with competitors, and sometimes the feature is a request (read: *mandate*) from the CEO. Frequently, I run into another answer that scares me even more: "A large consultancy advised us on what to do."

A company can pay a consultancy millions of dollars, but that still does not guarantee that the features it suggests are the right things to build. Teams that lock themselves into these plans of action before gathering actual evidence will build useless features that do not matter to their customers.

The dictionary defines *strategy* as "a plan of action or policy designed to achieve a major or overall aim." This definition seems to be the common interpretation of good strategy across businesses. Many companies spend months in "strategic planning" for the following year, creating comprehensive and detailed outlines of the tasks they will accomplish, the cost of those actions, and the revenue they will generate. This often is tied to the budgeting process, and teams must present business cases and timelines in order to secure funding for these projects.

Thinking of strategy as a plan is what gets us into the build trap. We keep adding new features to the list but have no way to evaluate whether they are the right features in the holistic context of our company. Stephen Bungay, one of the most respected leaders in strategy deployment and creation, has a different take on the concept of strategy. In his book on the subject, *The Art of Action*, he writes:

> *Strategy is a deployable decision-making framework, enabling action to achieve desired outcomes, constrained by current capabilities, coherently aligned to the existing context.*

A good strategy should transcend the iterations of features, focusing more on the higher-level goals and vision. A good strategy should sustain an organization for years. If you are changing strategy yearly or monthly, without good reason from data or the market, you are treating your strategy as a plan rather than as a framework.

11

Strategic Gaps

While studying strategy in many organizations, Stephen Bungay discovered that, when companies approach strategy as a plan, they often fail to achieve what they expected. This failure stems from the actions taken to fill the following gaps that exist between outcomes, plans, and actions. These gaps ultimately cause friction within the organization:

- The Knowledge Gap
- The Alignment Gap
- The Effects Gap

The Knowledge Gap

The Knowledge Gap (Figure 11-1) is the difference between what management would like to know and what the company actually knows. Organizations try to fill this gap by providing and demanding more detailed information.

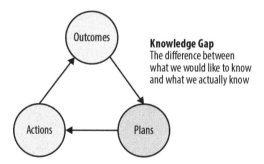

Figure 11-1. *The Knowledge Gap, by Stephen Bungay from the Art of Action (reprinted by permission of Hodder & Stoughton)*

If you're a leader saying to yourself, "Oh, damn, that's me," you are not alone. These were the exact words that popped out of the mouth of a CEO when I introduced this concept to him. This issue is probably the most readily recognizable of the gaps.

We also saw this gap surface with the CTO of Marquetly. He demanded that we lay out every single detail of a not-yet-validated product so that he could feel more certain about what we were doing. A deluge of information isn't always that helpful for upper management. You need to focus on communicating and asking for just enough information to make a decision.

Instead of seeking more detailed information, upper management should be limiting its direction to defining and communicating the *strategic intent*, or the goals of the business. The strategic intents combine to communicate where the company is heading and what it desires to achieve when it gets there. The strategic intent points the team toward the outcomes the businesses wants to achieve.

In the case with Marquetly, there were too many unknowns at the time to make a detailed plan. It still did not understand why users were falling off at certain steps of the sign-up flow. This was the core problem it needed to understand before coming up with the right solution. The company needed room to experiment and to understand *why* before it could suggest *how* to solve the problem.

Consider a product manager telling you the following: "I'm building this because it's going to help increase acquisitions, and new customer-acquisition is our big goal to drive the revenue prioritized at the corporate level. I know my product can bring people in. We know there's a problem here, but we're not sure what it is yet. Our next step is to discover that problem, tackle it with a solution, and then try to optimize the solution so we can increase acquisition." That's someone telling the story. A product manager who told you this should inspire confidence. Unfortunately, the opposite is usually true.

Leaders will still go through the ranks demanding more detailed information. Often, this is perceived as a lack of trust, and often it is, but there's usually something more there. In every organization where I've seen leaders operate this way, the story is not complete. Typically, there's a lack of alignment, and the goals of the team do not line up to an overall vision and strategy of the company. This Alignment Gap is what truly causes the demand for more and more information.

The Alignment Gap

The Alignment Gap, shown in Figure 11-2, is the difference between what people do and what management wants them to do, which is to achieve the business goals. Organizations try to fill this gap by providing more detailed instruction; whereas, instead, they should allow each level within the company to define how it will achieve the intent of the next level up.

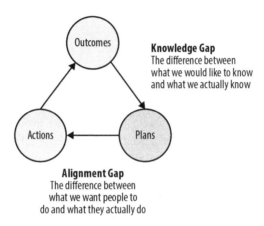

Knowledge Gap
The difference between
what we would like to know
and what we actually know

Alignment Gap
The difference between
what we want people to
do and what they actually do

Figure 11-2. *The Alignment Gap, by Stephen Bungay from the Art of Action (reprinted by permission of Hodder & Stoughton)*

At one company, I walked around asking all of the product managers on the hundred or so teams why they were working on their current project. I then asked their leaders the same question. I got two different answers from these two different levels. They could not connect the activities of the teams back to the outcomes of the companies because leadership had passed down feature requests rather than expected outcomes and goals. As soon as those feature requests were committed, it was nearly impossible to change them because the company expected them to be delivered.

Although I've witnessed this at many companies, there is one example that always haunts me. I was training product managers at a very large and established company (let's call it Company B), when I was told that it could not do any validation work around its products because the solutions the teams were building were already committed to the leadership of the company. Why? Well, Company B had hired a huge consulting firm to explore and dictate its product roadmap for the next five years. The consultants pored over market research and competitive analyses and came up with a roadmap, which then trickled down to the teams.

These teams, meanwhile, had been talking to customers and knew that these solutions the consultants had come up with were not what customers wanted. Yet their performance reviews were based on delivering those products. They wanted to do right by the customer, but they couldn't, for fear of losing their jobs. And so they built the wrong thing—knowingly. At the end of the year, Company B missed all of its goals, and the teams were penalized, even though they delivered on their roadmaps.

When these teams realized that customers did not want the consultant-proposed solution, they should have had the freedom to explore alternative options. That is how a product-led organization would operate. This is what keeps us out of the build trap. Instead, their adherence to predetermined meetings and formalities trapped them into staying quiet. Product teams need the freedom to explore solutions and to adjust their actions according to the data they receive. As long as they are aligned with the overall strategic intents and vision for the company, management should feel comfortable granting the necessary autonomy to capable teams.

Instead of sending down mandates, organizations should, instead, turn to aligning every level of the company around the *why* and should give the next layer down the opportunity to figure out the *how* and report back. When done this way, product management is successful. When leadership is not aligned at the top, the issues trickle all the way down to the teams. The lack of meaning and focus spreads, and, at the end of the year, the company will look at their target goals and ask, "What happened?" Lack of leadership alignment is by far the biggest issue I see standing in the way of successful product management.

The Effects Gap

The Effects Gap (Figure 11-3) is the difference between what we expect our actions to achieve and what actually happens. When organizations do not see the results they want, they try to fill this gap by putting more controls in place. However, that is the worst thing you can do in this scenario. Giving individuals and teams the freedom to adjust their actions so that they are in line with their goals is what will truly allow them to achieve results.

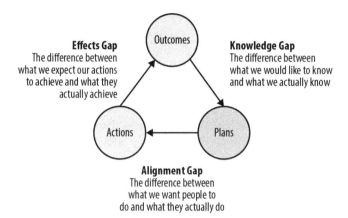

Figure 11-3. *The Effects Gap, by Stephen Bungay from the Art of Action (reprinted by permission of Hodder & Stoughton)*

All of these misguided, knee-jerk reactions start to pile up. Instead of aligning a team with a framework of goals and direction and then stepping back to give that team the room to explore how to reach the goals, management usually swings a complete 180 degrees. It asks for more information. It expects teams to commit to what management wants to do over the next year. It prescribes fully thought-out solutions, and then product teams are restricted to only those parameters instead of being able to focus on learning and adjusting their decisions as they go.

To solve these various gaps and to deliver great products to your customers, you need to view strategy in a different way, and, as Bungay proposes, enable action to achieve results. But why do we care about strategy being something that enables action? Well, that is how you scale an organization—by enabling action through autonomous teams.

Autonomous Teams

At Marquetly, the product managers were very frustrated by their lack of autonomy. One experienced product manager told me, "I keep having leaders tell me to own the vision of my product, but I'm not allowed. My manager keeps handing me solutions. Every time I try to suggest something different, I'm shut down. When we went Agile, we were told that our Scrum teams were supposed to be autonomous. This is definitely not autonomy."

Talking to the leaders of Marquetly, I heard a different story. "Our product managers won't step up and own the product. I have to keep prescribing things for them, but it's because they don't take initiative."

It's an interesting dichotomy but a common one I've seen in companies stuck in the build trap. These are all symptoms of not having a good strategy framework that enables action. When teams are not aligned with a clear direction and goals, they cannot effectively make decisions. If they dare to try, much of the time, the leader steps in and says, "No, that's not right."

Autonomy is what allows organizations to scale. The alternative is hiring hundreds or thousands of middle managers that lead by authority, telling people what to do. As organizations grow to the thousands—or even tens of thousands—of employees, this becomes incredibly inefficient and costly. It also causes unnecessary layers in management and a lot of frustration. People end up unhappy, and unhappy people rarely produce great work.

Leading by authority is a relic of industrial-age methodologies—when low-skilled workers were supervised closely so that their output was maximized. In the world of software, we don't work this way. We're hiring incredibly smart people and paying them hundreds of thousands of dollars to make the decisions on how to grow companies by making complex software that customers love. When you have that sort of talent, you need to give them the room to make decisions so that you can get the full benefit of their knowledge and skill.

That's what a strategic framework promotes. If you're aligned coherently and you have a good strategic framework, you can then allow people to make decisions without a lot of management oversight.

12

Creating a Good Strategic Framework

Back at Marquetly, the CEO was making great progress on getting his product team set. He went out and hired an excellent chief product officer (CPO) named Jen. Jen had come from another e-learning company focused on training developers. It had scaled its platform successfully and had a great exit with a profitable IPO.

I was excited for Jen to join the team. She had led efforts around creating the strategy at her last company, and she brought all that knowledge to this space. In her first week, she began picking up on the same problems I saw.

"I went around to all the product managers in the organization and asked them why they were working on certain things. None of them could answer me," she said. "No goals, no direction. They are just reactively building requests from customers."

She kept asking. "Then I went to my peers in the leadership team and asked them what was the most important thing we could do as a company," continued Jen. "They all gave me different answers. It's pretty clear we're not aligned on what our strategy is or what we want to become as a company."

Boom. She hit the nail on the head—and after only a week. Marquetly was stuck in reactive mode. It prioritized big projects based on customer requests or contracts. It wasn't thinking strategically about how to grow the product.

Luckily, the leadership team of Marquetly had bought in on getting on the same page so that they could be a more powerful organization. "We want to lead the market, we don't want to play catch-up," Chris, the CEO, told me. He originally thought the issues were with the development teams. "They aren't going fast enough, they are slacking off." Chris was a huge fan of Objectives and Key Results (OKRs) and had implemented them throughout the company, but they were very output-oriented instead of outcome-oriented. "Ship the first version of the new teacher platform," was how one objective was described. And "Deliver by June 2018" was considered a key result. They weren't tied to any outcome—either business or user-oriented.

We reflected on the company's current strategy process and how it got to these goals. When the company went into its planning meetings in November, everyone would emerge with a list of features to build and then dole them out to the product managers. The product managers then were responsible for estimating the amount of time it would take to complete the features with their development counterparts. After reporting these estimates back to the leadership team, they would then plan the budget and organize the roadmap.

Goals were set on the leadership level, as well. They had revenue targets they were promising to investors, based on entering this enterprise market. There were usage metrics set to measure whether people continued to use the site. Every part of the organization was measuring something, and yet, for the past few years, the company was not meeting its goals. The revenue targets fell short. The teams could not deliver some of the promised features. What happened?

The company was not correctly deploying and creating strategy. The telltale signs were there—all things Jen picked up on in her first week. The leadership team was prioritizing the work itself, based on what it thought was right to build rather than on feedback from customers. It was reacting to the customers that screamed the loudest instead of evaluating whether those requests matched the strategic objectives. The morale of the company was low, and, because of that, employees were not producing.

So the company decided to change. It decided to create and deploy a strategy that would work with modern product management methods.

A good company strategy should be made up of two parts: the operational framework, or how to keep the day-to-day activities of a company moving; and the strategic framework, or how the company realizes the vision through product and service development in the market. Many companies confuse these two frameworks and treat them as one and the same. Although both are important, getting the strategic framework right is essential for developing great products and services. That's what we talk about in the next chapters, because it is what directly influences product management.

This strategic framework aligns the company's strategy and vision with the products that are developed by the teams. Having a strong company vision and product visions that align to the strategic framework helps companies avoid swirl in planning and execution. Those companies that are busy creating new visions and strategies every year often are thinking too much in the short term and aren't planning enough for the future.

Maybe you recognize this pattern. It's the same story every year. In November, the company goes into panic mode, running around like chickens with their heads cut off, trying to predict the future for the next year. Revenue, commitments to shareholders, and budgets all get set. The laundry list of features that need to be built piles up into detailed Gantt charts. And then January 1 hits, and they get to work. They work on these things for a year, reach the arbitrary deadline of December 31, and then stop to adopt their next strategy. Repeat this year after year, and you leave no room to take on long-term projects or strategies.

Tying budgeting, strategy, and product development to this artificial yearly time cycle only creates lack of focus and follow-through. Instead, companies should be continuously evaluating where they are and where they need to take action, and then fund those decisions.

Think of the major pieces of work you do that are actually *bets*. Henrik Kniberg, a former consultant at Spotify, explains that this is how Spotify thinks.[1] The company operates using something called DIBBs, which stands for Data, Insights, Beliefs, and Bets. The first three things, data, insight, and beliefs, inform a piece of work called a bet. The concept of thinking of initiatives as bets is powerful because it sets up a different type of expectation.

Spotify maintains innovation by not establishing mandates about what to build from a higher-up perspective. Managers give employees the leeway to participate in hackathons and to implement their ideas. They set up an environment in which it's safe to try new things and fail. Upper management is willing to embrace uncertainty about what customers want, and, by doing so, they create a work environment that embraces experimentation and innovation and that can course-correct quickly, when necessary.

When strategy is communicated well in an organization, product development and management are synchronized. The company strategy informs the activities of the product development teams, and the execution of work on the products and data this produces informs the company direction. This should be a cyclical process throughout the organization, in which information is being communicated up, down, and across, to ensure alignment and understanding.

---

1 Henrik Kniberg, "Spotify Rhythm," talk at Agile Sverige, June 2016. *http://bit.ly/2qhTPL9*.

Strategy Deployment

Strategies are interconnecting stories told throughout the organization that explain the objective and outcomes, tailored to a specific time frame. We call this act of communicating and aligning those narratives *strategy deployment.*

Jabe Bloom, the founder of consulting firm PraxisFlow, works with executives to create and deploy strategies at large organizations. He explains why we should think about different levels of strategies as stories at different time scales:

> *At different levels of organizations, we tell stories with different scales of time (timespans), about our work and why we are doing it. In order for people to act on the stories they hear, the stories can't have significantly different time scales than they are accustomed to. Agile teams are really good at telling two- to four-week stories. That's what they deal with on a daily basis. As you go up in the organization, you tell stories with longer timespans. Executives are really good at telling five-year stories, but a team cannot act on a five-year story when they're used to thinking in two to four weeks. There's too much space to explore.*

Strategy deployment is about setting the right level of goals and objectives throughout the organization to narrow the playing field so that teams can act. So, while executives might be looking at a five-year strategy, middle management is thinking in smaller strategies—yearly or quarterly—bounding the teams in a direction that allows them to make decisions on a monthly or weekly basis.

When teams are not sufficiently constrained, they become stuck. As Bloom explains:

> *The unconstrained team is the most frightened and scared to act in the organization. They feel like they cannot make a decision because there are too many options. Appropriately constrained teams, ones who have a direction set to the right level for them, feel safe to make decisions because they can see how their stories align to the goals and structure of the organization.*

Not having the right level of direction lands us in the build trap. Teams are given instructions that are either too prescriptive or too broad. Executives will get too far into the weeds, managing by authority and not allowing autonomy. Or teams could, as Bloom mentioned, be given so much freedom they are unable to act. That is why strategy deployment is key, from a product development perspective.

There are many examples of strategy deployment across organizations. OKRs is a type of strategy deployment used by Google. Hoshin Kanri is a strategy deployment method used by Toyota. Even the military uses strategy deployment with mission command. All of these are based on the same premise—setting the direction for each level of an organization so they can act. Choosing the right framework is important for the organization, but understanding what makes a good strategy framework is even more important.

In most product organizations, there should be four major levels in strategy deployment (see Figure 12-1):

- Vision
- Strategic intent
- Product initiatives
- Options

Strategy Deployment

Vision	What do we want to be in 5-10 years? Value for customers, position in market, what our business looks like	CEO/Senior leadership
Strategic intent	What business **challenges** are standing in our way of reaching our vision?	Senior leadership Business leads
Product initiative	What **problems** can we address to tackle the challenge from a product perspective?	Product leadership team
Options	What are the different **ways** I can address those problems to reach my goals?	Product dev teams

Figure 12-1. *Strategy deployment levels*

The first two are at the company level, whereas the last two are specific to the products or services of the company. Strategy deployment and strategy creation, though, are two different things. A significant amount of work goes into defining what each of these should be, coordinating them across product lines and teams and then communicating them upward and downward for buy in.

Strategy Creation

Strategy creation is the process of figuring out which direction the company should act upon and of developing the framework in which people make decisions. Strategies are created at each level and then deployed across the organization.

If you do not already have a strategy in place, I want to stress that this is *not* a one-day or one-week process. I have seen companies try to cram the creation of a strategy into that time frame and fail. This is something that takes time and focus to craft and maintain. You need to be identifying problems and determining how to organize around solving them at every level of strategy. If you are in the C-Suite, getting this right should be your top priority—or you'll be setting up your hundreds or thousands of employees for failure.

Strategy is about how you take the organization from where you currently are and reach the vision. For strategy to be created, you must first understand the vision, or where you want to go. Then we can identify problems or obstacles standing in our way of getting there and experiment around tackling them. We repeatedly do this until we reach the vision.

This is the basis of the continuous improvement framework practiced at Toyota, called the Improvement Kata, which helped it determine its strategies. The Kata teaches people in the company how to strategically tackle problems to reach goals. Mike Rother documented how the process works in his book, *Toyota Kata*, an excerpt of which you can see in Figure 12-2.

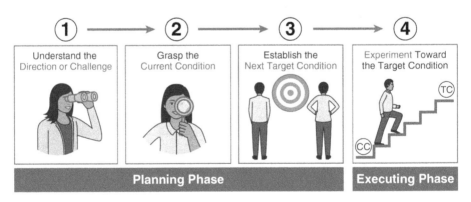

Figure 12-2. *"The Four Steps to the Improvement Kata" from Toyota Kata Practice Guide, by Mike Rother (reprinted by permission of Mike Rother)*

During the Plan Do Check Act (PDCA) cycles —in step 4, teams go through and systematically identify obstacles standing in the way of reaching the target condition, their next goal, plan out how to tackle it, and then experiment in order to see whether the plan worked. They then reflect on the progress (check) and act accordingly in the next round.

With product development, you can harness this same approach, but we need to customize it to your situation. I call this the Product Kata, as illustrated in Figure 12-3.

The Product Kata

A scientific, systematic way to build better products
by Melissa Perri

Figure 12-3. *The Product Kata, by Melissa Perri*

To understand the direction, you are looking at either the vision, strategic intent, or product initiative, depending on which level you are starting on. The current state is related to where you stand in relation to your vision. It also reflects the current state of the outcomes, including the current measurement of those outcomes.

Option goals are our next level of goals from the team. These are the outcomes you need to achieve in order to make progress toward your initiative or intent. Then you conduct your product process to experiment around systematically tackling problems to reach your goal. We dive more into the product management process in Part IV.

Through this act of exploring and identifying problems, you uncover data that is needed to help inform the strategy and vision. Vision is not set solely top-down by management. The entire organization should be sharing information as they learn about what will reach goals, and help inform the strategy. Bloom calls this Information Physics:

> One of the biggest issues I hear from executives is that they do not have the data they need to make decisions. People ask them to create a vision, but they do not continuously surface information in a way that helps inform the strategic decisions that enable the organization to achieve the vision. The teams should be out there, analyzing, testing, and learning and then communicating what they discover back to their peers and their management teams. This is how we set strategy.

This process of communicating data and direction up and down—and across—the organization is how we maintain alignment. But it needs to first start at the company level.

13

Company-Level Vision and Strategic Intents

Company Vision

The company vision is the linchpin in the strategy architecture. It sets the direction and provides meaning for everything that follows. Having a strong company vision gives you a framework around which to think about your products.

Amazon is an example of a company with a great vision and strategy, both of which serve its products well. On its website, Amazon notes that its company vision is, "to be Earth's most customer-centric company, where customers can find and discover anything they might want to buy online, and endeavors to offer its customers the lowest possible prices."

The company is made up of many different product lines, from its Prime Video service to Fulfillment to Amazon. Each one of its products helps Amazon to achieve its overall vision, by creating a better experience for people who are shopping. By keeping an eye on the overall vision, the product people who test, develop, and grow these different products are able to make effective decisions about what they should and shouldn't pursue.

If you are a single-product company, like Roku, this is easy because your company vision is very similar, if not the same, as your product vision. If you are a large corporation, like Bank of America, it becomes complex. The strategy needs to start at the corporate level, moving through the business lines, and ultimately arriving at the products. In these types of companies, products are just details on how the company vision is manifested. They are the vehicles for value —the things you sell to customers, while receiving some form of value in return. Here the company vision is the wrapper that gives meaning to all of the products and services you offer.

Now you might be thinking, "What is the difference between a company mission and vision?" A good *mission* explains why the company exists. A *vision*, on the other hand, explains where the company is going based on that purpose. I find that the best thing a company can do is to combine both the mission and the vision into one statement to provide the value proposition of the company—what the company does, why it does it, and how it wins doing that. Here are a few examples of compelling vision statements:

> *To offer designer eyewear at a revolutionary price, while leading the way for socially conscious businesses.*
>
> **—WARBY PARKER**

> *At Bank of America, we are guided by a common purpose to help make financial lives better by connecting clients and communities to the resources they need to be successful.*
>
> **—BANK OF AMERICA**

> *Becoming the best global entertainment distribution service, licensing entertainment content around the world, creating markets that are accessible to film makers, and helping content creators around the world to find a global audience.*
>
> **—NETFLIX**

All of these vision statements provide focus for the company. They are short, memorable, and clearly articulated. They also don't include fluffy terminology.

Many companies create a vision statement that is something like, "To be the market leader in online photo storage." Although that's a good thing to strive for, it leaves the rest of the company asking how and why. It's too broad. I don't want to get overprescriptive on the *how* here, but you do need to focus your company around where you want to concentrate.

Take Netflix. Although it said it wanted to be the best global entertainment distribution service, it provided focus on how the company planned to do that—by licensing content around the world, creating markets that are accessible, and helping content creators. It's okay to want to be the best or the market leader, but you need to give some context on how.

If your vision has been murky for a while, you need to provide more than just a vision statement. Company leaders need to spend time communicating their vision, explaining their choices, and painting an image of what is to come. This doesn't mean that you need to get super-detailed about how this all manifests. It just means that you must tell a story. When that story is told, you can remind everyone through the simple vision statement.

Going back to Marquetly, it had a compelling and well-stated vision already: "We grow digital marketing professionals by giving them access to quality training across a wide array of topics in an engaging way designed to maximize learning in a short amount of time."

It explains why the company exists and what it does to accomplish that purpose. The executive team at Marquetly did excellent work crafting the vision statement to anchor the team. Although the vision is clear, the difficult part is connecting it back to the company's operations. This is where it's necessary for company leaders to specify *strategic intents*. These few, concise, outcome-oriented goals focus the company around how to reach the vision.

Strategic Intents

Although the vision should remain stable over a long period of time, how you intend to reach that vision changes as your company matures and develops. Strategic intents communicate the company's current areas of focus that help realize the vision. Strategic intents usually take a while to reach, on the magnitude of one to several years.

Strategic intents are always aligned to the current state of the business. When determining what these intents are, the C-Suite of the company should ask, "What is the most important thing we can do to reach our vision, based on where we are now?" There should not be laundry list of desires or goals—just a few key things that need to happen to make a big leap forward. Keeping the list of strategic intents small focuses everyone.

This is where Marquetly, like many companies out there, struggled. Every year, it would go into a yearly planning cycle to talk about the things the company wanted to do in the upcoming year. This was usually a meeting with senior leadership, reserved only for VPs or more senior leaders. At that time, attendees would come up with a list of product features. For example, last year's list had the ability to share classes with others, referral codes, a new way to conduct quizzes, and a leaderboard for the entire site. These ideas were usually thought up by the senior leadership team and then communicated down to the product teams that were tasked with execution.

Although not bad ideas, these solutions were at a much lower feature level than the C-Suite should be concerned with. Instead of dictating these solutions down to the teams, leadership should have been focused on creating strategic intents. This approach would have aligned the decision making at the product level with the goals of the business and would have helped the company move solidly in one direction. Instead, they were peanut buttering—spreading themselves thin over many areas of work instead of making a concerted push in one direction.

I held a strategy session for Marquetly's leaders to align on where they really wanted to go. To understand how to set our strategic intents, we had to first understand what business value really means. Joshua Arnold, a business and product consultant and expert on cost of delay, uses a great model for thinking about business value,[1] as shown in Figure 13-1.

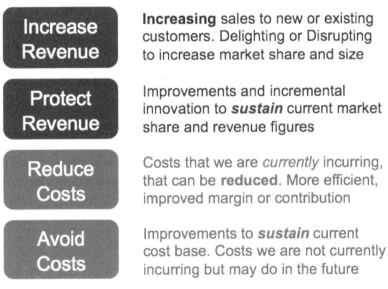

Figure 13-1. *Framework for thinking about value, by Joshua Arnold (reprinted by permission of Joshua Arnold, © 2002)*

When organizations plan their strategic intents, they should think about how each part of the organization can contribute to these goals. For growing companies, increasing revenue is going to be the most important bucket on here. But

1 *http://bit.ly/2OONGoC*

for larger enterprises, you should be evaluating initiatives across the company in each area.

Marquetly was focused on increasing revenue. Its strategic intents mostly fell into that category, since they had to grow quickly from $50 million in revenue to $150 million in the next few years in order to IPO. This was the kind of return its investors were looking for. The company analyzed what it was currently doing and how much it thought it could gain by focusing the organization around areas for revenue growth.

Marquetly realized that, in order to grow its revenue to the numbers it needed, it should focus on expanding upmarket, selling to larger companies (enterprises), which currently made up a small portion of its revenue. This would allow Marquetly to sell licenses in bulk, producing more revenue and fostering greater retention, as the few enterprises that already used Marquetly's product tended to renew annually. The company also realized that, to reach its revenue goals, it would need to increase the revenue from individual users, as well. At that point, its acquisition rates were not great. Management set these as the company's two strategic intents and associated the appropriate revenue goals around them, as illustrated in Table 13-1.

Table 13-1. *Marquetly's strategic intents*

Intent	Goals
Expand into the enterprise business.	Increase revenue from currently $5 million a year to $60 million a year in three years.
Double revenue growth from individual users.	Increase revenue growth from 15% YoY to 30% YoY from individual users.

Getting the right level and number of strategic intents is incredibly important. As Marquetly found out before, too many higher-level goals, and you are back to peanut buttering. I once saw a company with 5,000 people have 80 strategic intents. With 5,000 people, they shipped only one feature per quarter because everyone was wildly distracted and working on too many things. One intent is usually good for a small company, and three are plenty for a large organization. Yes, three. I know that sounds like very few goals for an organization of thousands of people, but that is key. This is also where the level and time frame matter.

Strategic intents should be at a high level and business focused. They are about entering new markets, creating new revenue streams, or doubling down in certain areas. Think back to the Netflix example at the beginning of this section.

Netflix had a clear strategic intent: "Lead the streaming market." All of its deci-sions, from enabling internet-connected devices to focusing on creating more content for users, helped to achieve this goal. It pushed them in the right direc-tion. When that goal was realized, Netflix changed course to maintain its position by creating its own content—another strategic intent. These are not small goals. They need an army to execute, from product development to marketing to con-tent creation. That's the point. The strategic intents are about the whole com-pany, not just the product solution.

Marquetly became aligned around the two biggest things it could accomplish to reach its goals, as depicted in Figure 13-2.

Marquetly   **INTENT DEEP DIVE**

Strategic Intent

> **Double Revenue Growth from Individual Users**
>
> Increase revenue growth from 15% YoY to 30% YoY from individual users.

Product Initiative

We believe that by increasing the amount of content on our site in key areas of interest, we can acquire more individual users and retain existing users, resulting in a potential revenue increase of $2,655,000 per month from individual users.	We believe that by creating a way for students to prove their skills to prospective or current employers, we can increase acquisition, resulting in a revenue increase of $1,500,000 a month.

Figure 13-2. *Marquetly strategic intent and product initiative*

Marquetly put in the work and was able to set its strategic intents after a two-month process, with the executive team checking back in biweekly. Then the question became how the entire company could rally around these intents and crush it. And how, from a product development perspective, could they prioritize the work to win? This is where the product initiatives are defined and are aligned to the product visions.

14

Product Vision and Portfolio

Product initiatives translate the business goals into the problems that we will solve with our product. The product initiatives answer *how*? How can I reach these business goals by optimizing my products or building new ones?

With Netflix, the biggest thing it needed to do to really get streaming to take off was to enable people to watch Netflix on any device, wherever viewers wanted to. Think about it. At the time, if you wanted to download something, you could watch it only on your laptop. There were no internet-connected devices. And no one wants to watch TV on their tiny laptop screen all the time. First of all, you're basically saying that no one can watch it with you. And second, a 13-inch screen is hardly a cinematic experience.

Netflix created a product initiative to tackle this problem for the user. Putting that in user story format, we'd get, "As a Netflix subscriber, I want to be able to watch Netflix anywhere, with anyone, comfortably." This is the company's product initiative. It then explored many possible solutions—developing the Roku, partnering with Xbox and creating an app for it, and ultimately enabling all the internet-connected devices it could. All of these solutions, which I call *options*, were aligned to this product initiative.

Options are your bets, as Spotify would call them. They represent the possible solutions that teams will explore to solve the product initiative. Now, sometimes the solution will be readily apparent or easy to understand, based on best practices or previous work, but other times you will need to experiment to find the solution.

Product initiatives set the direction for the product teams to explore options. They tie the goals of the company back to a problem we can solve for the users or customers. Product managers are in charge of making sure the product initiatives and options are aligned with the vision of an existing product or portfolio. Sometimes, you might even end up creating new products to solve these problems for your users. The product vision and portfolio vision keep you anchored in the problems and solutions that you want to explore.

Product Vision

In the past two years, I have met with more than a dozen companies that have had trouble aligning around a *product vision*. They built products for the past decade and have reached a point at which they can no longer scale. All of them have the same problem: too many products and no coherent vision. They were building one-off products to satisfy individual customer requests, but they failed to address a wider audience. Or they built products that helped them move into new markets but did not figure out how these new products reconciled with their existing offerings. Many of these companies are ridiculously successful—they make over a billion dollars a year—but they are bogged down with too many people, little direction, and no holistic approach, making it difficult to keep growing.

Although having a strategy usually helps these companies align and focus their work, it also reveals a bigger issue: the lack of an overall product vision. Even though having multiple features and ways to deliver value is a good thing, we need something to tie it all together at the top.

The product vision communicates why you are building something and what the value proposition is for the customer. Amazon does this particularly well by creating what they call Press Release documents for every product vision. These short (typically a page or two) notices describe the problem the user is facing and how the solution enables the user to solve that problem.

The product vision emerges from experimentation around solving problems for users. After you validate that the solution is the right one, you can grow it into a scalable, maintainable product. But you need to be careful not to make the product vision too specific. It cannot describe every little feature but should include more of the main capabilities it enables for the user. If you are too prescriptive, it could stifle the way you grow the product and what you might add to it later.

At Marquetly, the company was formulating the product vision for their products. They had many students already on the platform, and it was beginning to take shape. The direction was validated, but the company needed to pull together what it did in a cohesive statement. Jen led them around an exercise to arrive at this vision:

We help marketing professionals to advance their skills by allowing them to understand their current competencies, easily find the most relevant classes to get to the next level, and then learn the skills they need in the most engaging and digestible fashion, from world-class teachers in the marketing space.

This simple statement describes the problem the user is trying to solve and the capabilities it enables for them to solve it. It does not get into specific details on the features but focuses more on the qualities that are important to the user: ease of use, relevance, and engagement. You can start to paint a picture of how this product now works, along with the needed and the components. There's an assessment, something that tells the user which classes to take, and then a way to take a class and understand whether user skills improved. This is a good starting point that helps the company organize its teams and understand scope.

The VP of product usually is the one who owns the product vision, but they might not be the first one to set it. As I said, products emerge out of experimentation, so usually a smaller team is responsible for determining what that product looks like. As the product becomes more robust, you build a team around it to grow it. But the VP of product should make sure everyone is aligned to this holistic vision.

In companies with one product, the product initiatives describe the major user problems that the company is prioritizing. They need to be aligned to both the product initiative and the strategic intents. The VP of product works with the product managers below them to determine which are the right problems to solve to achieve both of these things. Sometimes, one of the problems that should be solved does not relate directly to the product vision. This is where a company would decide to introduce a new product and to create a product portfolio.

Product Portfolio

Companies with more than one product often wrap their products under what is called a *product portfolio*. Very large companies have multiple product portfolios, all aligned by the type of value they provide to customers. For example, Adobe has the Adobe Creative Cloud as a product portfolio, which consists of the applications Photoshop, Illustrator, and InDesign, among others. It also has another product portfolio for next-generation applications, consisting of newer creative tools, such as those for rapid prototyping.

The chief product officer (CPO) is responsible for setting the direction and overseeing the product portfolio. Having a philosophy for how your products or services help your company reach that vision in the near term or long term is key. To get there, the CPO answers these questions for their team:

- How do all of our products work as a system to provide value to our customers?
- What unique value does each of the product lines offer that makes this a compelling system?
- What overall values and guidelines should we consider when deciding on new product solutions?
- What should we stop doing or building because it does not serve this vision?

The product initiatives emerge from the work that needs to be done across the product portfolio to achieve the strategic intents and to further the individual product visions. This is also where you want to make sure that you are balancing the work of the teams with the direction of the company. The CPO is responsible for figuring out how to balance these areas of work in a framework.

For the portfolio, you need to look at all of the things that need to be accomplished to balance your investments, the number of people, and the capacity you're putting into each area in order to achieve success across the board. One thing this approach also helps with is finding time for innovation. Leaders always complain that they don't have time to innovate. Usually, this is due to poor capacity planning and strategy creation.

It's not that you don't have time to innovate; it's that you are not *making time* to innovate. To find that space, you're going to need to say no to some things. We're all bogged down by work, and there are always a million things you could be doing that will pay off tomorrow. If you want to be innovative, you actually need to dedicate teams to this and make space in your portfolio to make sure that all of this happens.

Amazon is the king of building innovation into its portfolio. It spins up teams in secret labs, and these teams spend years figuring out how to expand the company's business. The Amazon Echo came out of such an initiative. The company dedicated an entire team to exploring how voice control can help people shop more. The product teams spent five more years exploring,[1] defining, and refining the Echo and Alexa voice control before it launched it to wild success. Amazon set the time and space aside that it needed in product initiatives to go after and explore how to enter this new market.

---

1 Eugene Kim, "The inside story of how Amazon created Echo, the next billion-dollar business no one saw coming," Business Insider. *https://read.bi/2Sk8OBa.*

PART IV

Product Management Process

ROLE
STRATEGY
PROCESS
ORGANIZATION

The best solutions are linked to real problems that users want solved. Product managers use a process to identify which of those problems the team can solve to further the business and achieve the strategy. Product managers can rely on the Product Kata to help them develop the right experimental mindset to fall in love with the problem rather than the solution. They continue iterating until they reach the outcome.

"Maybe we just need to offer a free account version, where people can try it before they buy it."

"No, I think we need to offer heavy discounts and we can get people to sign up for a few months."

"It's really just the quality of the teachers we have on our site. If we had bigger name teachers, we would get more students in."

We were in a heated debate at Marquetly about what could possibly drive more revenue from individual users. The team's strategic intent was to increase revenue from users. Everyone had an idea, and many of them were intriguing. Each idea could have been the right solution for a particular problem—except that we didn't understand what the problem was. Where were we experiencing issues? How could we drive more revenue? These were the things we needed to know more about.

"Wait!" I interjected. "Let's all take a step back and break down what we do know. Our goal is to increase revenue from individual users. I can think of three ways to do that, based on what we know from product metrics. What do you think?"

Monica, a product manager, chimed in. "Well, we can acquire new users. That will increase revenue."

"Exactly," I said. "What else? There are two more options."

Christa, another product manager, then hesitantly spoke up. "We could also retain our existing users better. Our retention rate is only at 40% over six months."

"Bingo. Retaining people will increase more lifetime value per person. There's one more."

"We could create new revenue streams for existing users. Try to find something to upsell," said Joe, our VP of product on student experience.

Those were our three choices:

- Acquire more individual users.
- Retain existing individual users better.
- Create new revenue streams for existing individual users.

"So we have to figure out where the problems and opportunities are surrounding each of those," I said. "For acquisition and retention, let's dig into the data and feedback we have and try to diagnose whether there are any issues there. For new revenue streams, let's discuss possible ideas."

The team set out to pull the data, splitting up into two groups. One team was analyzing the acquisition funnel, looking at every step a user took from the time they got on the site until they signed up. There the team found very low conversion rate from people who went on the site to those who actually signed up and paid.

"We see that we are doing well with marketing, but even with the discounts we already have, they aren't signing up. How do we figure out what is stopping them? We don't we have any of their information," said Monica.

"Have you heard of a tool called Qualaroo?" asked Rich, the lead developer. "It allows us to poll people when they go toward the back button or try to leave the page. We can ask them what's stopping them from signing up. I can easily add this to the site in about 10 minutes."

"That is awesome," said Monica. "Let's do it and see what we get."

The team put the Qualaroo widget on its site. Within a week, it had more than a hundred responses.

"It's amazing, we learned so much," said Monica. "And no one said they were leaving because of free trials!" It turned out that about 55% of the people said they were leaving because they couldn't find enough classes in new types of marketing methods, like social media. Another 25% said they were looking for something that could help them get into marketing as a career transition, but they didn't see how these classes proved they gained any skills.

"We do the assessment at the beginning when they sign up, but we never reassess them to show they've mastered any skills," said Monica. The other 20% of responses included a host of other themes but nothing substantial. "I think we found two big problems."

The other team was also fast at work exploring retention. "We found that only 40% of people stay with us after six months," Christa was explaining. "We followed up with 100 people who recently left and asked them why, and 90% of them said they ran out of content that was interesting to them. They had taken about 10 of our classes, but they didn't find enough on new ways of marketing. It was all the old standard stuff that they could learn anywhere—and sometimes for free on YouTube."

Now we had two groups of people—existing users and new users—both with the same problem. They were not finding the classes they wanted on the site, and there were not enough to justify them staying for longer than six months.

"We know we need more content, but how do we get it?" asked Karen. "Do we have the right teachers for this, or do we need to attract them? How much content are our teachers producing?" She was concerned about the teacher side of the business and decided to have Christa investigate.

Reaching out, Christa found that teachers were having trouble creating courses. Most of them had created only one, yet more than half of the current teachers wanted to create a new course but couldn't do so. The teachers had two problems: the platform was difficult to use, and they were not sure what students wanted. "Had I known they were interested in social media, I would have started there," said one of the teachers. The options and product initiatives were beginning to emerge. The team started putting them together.

Marquetly Product Initiatives

INITIATIVE 1

We believe that by increasing the amount of content on our site in key areas of interest, we can acquire more individual users and retain existing users, resulting in a potential revenue increase of $2,655,000 per month from individual users.

Options to explore

- Easier and faster ways for teachers to create courses
- Feedback loops for teachers on areas of interest for students
- Outreach to new teachers who can create courses in areas of interest

INITIATIVE 2

We believe that by creating a way for students to prove their skills to prospective or current employers, we can increase acquisition, resulting in a revenue increase of $1,500,000 a month.

Options to explore

- Continuous assessment that allows students to constantly take tests to prove skills
- Certificates of completion and competence

The team then brought these ideas to Jen for approval. When she gave the go-ahead, they broke up and began experimenting around how to achieve these goals.

This section is all about the process of uncovering the right thing to build. Usually, when we think about processes, we focus more on the act of developing software than we do about building the right software. This is the build trap. You can get out of the build trap by understanding and applying problem-solving and experimentation techniques like Marquetly's team did here to find what it should focus on. This is the product management process, and it starts with the Product Kata.

15

The Product Kata

As discussed earlier, and as seen in Figure 15-1, The Product Kata is the process by which we uncover the right solutions to build. It's a systematic way that teaches product managers to approach building products from a problem-solving standpoint. The Product Kata helps product people form incredibly impactful habits. Doing it over and over again, exactly like a martial arts kata, ingrains the process in your brain. After practicing for a while, this pattern of thought becomes second nature.

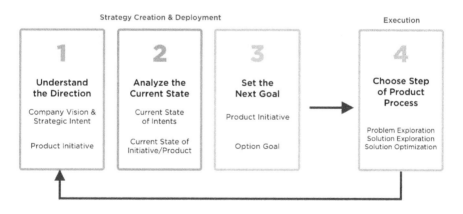

Figure 15-1. *The Product Kata, by Melissa Perri*

We go through these steps to uncover the product initiatives and the options.

The first task is to get to the product initiative. To do this, you need to understand the strategic intent, evaluate the current state of that strategic intent in relation to where your products can help, and determine what problems you can solve to further that strategic intent. This is what Marquetly did during its research and analysis to arrive at the product initiatives of increasing content and building out a more robust assessment.

There can be many options that help reach the product initiative, as we saw with the three we had to produce more content at Marquetly. One or all of these might be what it takes to get us to the successful outcome of the initiative, and that's okay. To determine whether we are getting closer to achieving our product initiative, we need to break the success metrics into something we can measure on a shorter time scale. We call this the *team goal*, and it's how we measure the success of the option. Although it can take six months or longer to reach the product initiative goal, the team goal should be something we can measure after every release, which gives us feedback that our option is working the way we want it to. We set the team goal with the same process as we did for the product initiative.

Context Matters

Since Lean Startup emerged on the scene, experimentation has been a hot button topic in many software companies. I see teams readily jump into experimenting, exciting to kick off that A/B test or to prototype something. It's important to take a step back and understand where you are and what is needed in that stage before you jump into any work. This is where the Product Kata helps.

After we have set the goal, we begin walking through the Product Kata. We ask ourselves the following:

1. What is the goal?

2. Where are we now in relation to that goal?

3. What is the biggest problem or obstacle standing in the way of me reaching that goal?

4. How do I try to solve that problem?

5. What do I expect to happen (hypothesis)?

6. What actually happened, and what did we learn?

We do answer questions one through four to figure out how to plan our next move as a team. Then we reflect on that work in questions five and six and determine whether to go back to the beginning for the next round. These questions take us through the problem exploration, solution exploration, and solution optimization phases. The steps we choose to take and the tools we implement to do so will change, depending on where we are.

It's important to understand each phase so that we are doing just enough to get us to the goal. One of the biggest mistakes I've seen in product management is teams rushing in to apply a tool or practice at the wrong stage. Many times, they are experimenting unnecessarily when the problem is not yet known or when there is already a good idea about the solution.

When considering whether to experiment around a particular solution, I think of what my friend Brian Kalma, former head of UX for Zappos, once told me: "Don't spend your time overdesigning and creating unique, innovative solutions for things that are not core to your value proposition. If someone has already solved that problem with a best practice, learn from that, implement their solutions, gather data to determine if it's successful in your situation, and then iterate. Reserve your time and energy for the things that will make or break your value proposition."

A good example of this is a checkout page on an e-commerce website. If you don't want to get into the business of being a checkout service for other e-commerce companies, don't spend all your time here. There's lots of experimentation that has already happened around this particular solution, and you can harness that. I should know. I researched this heavily when I worked at an e-commerce company. If you can, learn from those who have optimized already, implement their best practices, and tweak from there. When that's not an option, you have a chance to explore adjacent areas or to chart your own path.

When the problem that you are solving is core to your value proposition, take a step back and don't rush into the first solution. Use your unique context to set you apart from competitors. Experiment with a few solution ideas before committing to one.

With this approach to product management, all design and development work is in service to reaching a goal. It doesn't mean that all of the things you try will be shipped. Hopefully, many of them won't be. The best thing you can do, at this point, is kill the bad ideas! The fewer features, the better. That is how you reduce the complexity of products. Otherwise, you can quickly run into feature fatigue from customers. Remember, it's about quality, not quantity. The tasks of focusing on the Product Kata and identifying which phase you are in and what tools are available there are key to successful product management. In the next few chapters, we talk about how to go through each of these phases:

1. Understanding the direction
2. Problem exploration
3. Solution exploration
4. Solution optimization

16

Understanding the Direction and Setting Success Metrics

At Marquetly, I was working with the VPs of product, Karen and Joe, and we were figuring out how to quantify their product initiative in order to take it to Jen.

"Now let's go back over the data that we already have," I suggested. "What are our current retention and acquisition rates?"

Joe pulled up the data that the team had gathered during its exploration of product initiatives. "We currently retain users at a rate of 40% after six months. That isn't great."

"No, that's definitely not great because we're also planning to spend more acquiring users in the coming months. That means we'll be burning through some money if we can't retain them," said Karen.

"Okay, so we know those numbers. Now let's look at our problem. We found that users wanted more course variety. What percentage of them, roughly, do we think want that?" I asked them.

"Well," Karen said, "we have two points of data we can pull from to approximate that. We left Qualaroo running on our site for about a month, and we're finding that, of the people who answered, about 55% of them said they were looking for more course variety. We now have statistical significance around that number, too. So that means we are potentially losing out on 82,500 people every month signing up. Not all of those people are going to convert, but the upside to solving this problem is high."

"And that's only part of the potential, too," I said. "Let's look at those numbers for retention."

"We polled the people who left recently, and 90% of them said there were not enough courses to interest them. We looked at our churn numbers, and based on those, we're losing $180,000 a month in revenue. Not as much as the potential acquisition but still an issue." Joe shrugged a bit.

"Now, we know not everyone will be retained at 100%, and we know that the acquisition rate isn't going to be completely at 100% of those people who didn't sign up. But we can start to set acquisition and revenue goals from the data. So let's think about what is realistic," I said. "What do you think we can feasibly affect with these numbers?"

"Well, if we increase the retention rate from 40% to 70%, we will be gaining $90,000 a month in revenue. If we double our acquisition rate, we can get a little over $7 million a year more. That brings us to a total of just over $8 million a year, which would bring us very close to that 30% goal of revenue growth with our strategic intent."

Karen wrote down the initiative to present to Jen:

We believe that, by increasing the amount of content on our site in key areas of interest, we can double acquisition and increase our retention of existing users to 70%, resulting in a potential revenue increase of $8 million a year from individual users.

"I like this," Jen said. "We can see that there is value in adding more content —the feedback is clear there. This initiative gets us about halfway to our goal of increasing revenue for the individual users. I'm willing to invest in it. What are you thinking around hypotheses so far?"

"We have a couple of ideas," Joe responded. "One, we believe we can target new teachers who are experts specifically in content areas the students are asking for. We're going to leverage the marketing team to help us reach out to prospective teachers, but we'll have a small team exploring the right types of content and profiles to target for the teachers. Two, we have a team exploring what is preventing current teachers from creating more courses. We have lots of qualified teachers, but they have only made one course. The product managers and UX designers are researching those areas, while the teams are finishing up the next release."

"Great! Let me know when you have more data on direction," said Jen. "This is all looking good so far." Jen approved. Joe and Karen went to tell the teams that they had the go-ahead to fully explore their options around this initiative. After they had clearer direction, they would update Jen.

Karen went over to Christa, the product manager on the teacher experience, to give her the news and set her up to explore the issues with her team.

"We're going to walk through the Product Kata in order to set you up for success. So, first, you need to identify your obstacles or customer problems standing in the way of teachers creating more content. Let's regroup in a week and see what you've found around that."

Christa enlisted the help of their UX designer and lead engineer to dive deeper. She started off by going over their product initiative and helping them understand how they got there. Then she explained what they already knew:

"When we did the initial research, we found that a lot of the students were interested in learning new marketing methods. These were things like harnessing social media and content creation to drive traffic to the site. So it's not enough just to increase content—we have to be strategic about it. We've been getting feedback for months from teachers emailing us for help. A lot of the questions are around how to upload information more quickly, and there seems to be a very clumsy workflow. I'm trying to figure out how widespread the issue is so we can quantify it. What can we do to get data on how many people experience this problem?"

"I can set up a quick open-ended survey with a text box for our teachers and ask what is preventing them from doing a second course," said the UX designer, Matt.

"I can pull session times out of the system from when people start a course and when they complete it. We have event timing around this," Rich, the lead developer said.

"Great! Let's take a week and investigate as much as we can. At the end, we can pull together the data and see if this is something worth diving deeper into."

The team got to work. Early the next week, everyone got back together to go over the findings. I met up with them to go through their results.

"It's bad," Matt said. "I didn't realize how poorly the experience was designed, and the teachers sound incredibly frustrated. It takes them on average, a month to put together a course, even when they have most of the content already developed. We're missing a ton of the features that they would like, such as audio-only lessons, bringing in outside content, and linking out to more articles. Plus, it's very buggy. There's a lot we can do around here to improve the experience, and the teachers really would love to create more courses."

"Yeah, I found similar information in the databases and event records," said Rich. "On average, it takes a teacher 61 days from the day they start a course until they publish one. Over 75% of the teachers who start a course never publish it. I think some of the issues that Chris discovered could be causing it."

"Hmm, this is good information," I said. "Now think about what can result from improving this experience that will lead to more course creation. You need to identify your leading indicators."

"There are a few things we can look to improve if we tackle this experience," said Christa. "We can increase the rate of published courses, and we can increase the number of second courses created by teachers."

"Perfect," I said. They were doing really well. "Now you have to baseline those numbers and pull them together into an option statement."

The team pulled together the numbers from the data and defined their original option statement:

> We believe that, by making it faster and easier for teachers to create courses, we can increase the rate of published courses to 50% and increase the number of second courses created to 30%.

Christa brought it back to Karen, who responded, "You need to get a bit more firm around what this actually entails, but I like this direction. When you get deeper into your problem and solution exploration, let's revisit this and see if we can add more color around what exactly we can build or do to make those numbers go up."

Now the team was ready to start its problem exploration and to dive deeper into what was frustrating the teachers.

Product Metrics

Product metrics tell you how healthy your product is, and, ultimately, your business, given that a healthy product contributes to overall health of the business. They are the lifeblood of every product manager. Keeping a pulse on your product is crucial for knowing when you should act and where. This is how we set direction.

But it's easy to become stuck measuring the wrong things. Frequently, teams turn to measuring what we call *vanity metrics*. This concept, introduced in Lean Startup, is about goals that look shiny and impressive because they always get bigger. People are excited to share how many users are on their product, how many daily page views they have, or how many logins their system has. Although these numbers may make you look great to investors, they do not help product teams or businesses make decisions. They do not cause you to change your behavior or priorities.

You can easily turn a vanity metric into an actionable metric by adding a time component to it. Do you have more users this month than last? What did you do differently? Think carefully about how to add context and meaning to your facts and figures. Consider the meaning behind the metrics and how they help inform your decisions and understanding.

In addition to vanity metrics, I often see product teams measuring output-oriented metrics, such as the number of features shipped, story points complete, or user stories worked on. Although these are good productivity metrics, they are not product metrics. They cannot tie the results of product development back to the business. So we need a set of metrics that can help us do that.

There are many product frameworks available to help you think through the appropriate product goals. My two favorites are Pirate Metrics and HEART metrics.

Pirate Metrics

Pirate Metrics were created by Dave McClure, founder of 500 Startups, to talk about the life cycle of users through your product. Think of it as a funnel (Figure 16-1): users finding your product is *acquisition*; users having a great first experience is *activation*; keeping users returning to your product is called *retention*; users recommending others because they love your product is *referral*; and, finally, users paying for your product because they see value in it is *revenue*. Put it all together and you get AARRR—Pirate Metrics. Get it?

Figure 16-1. *Pirate Metrics, by Dave McClure*

The difference between activation and acquisition is usually the most difficult to understand on this framework. Acquisition is that users land on your site and sign up. This is what they were measuring at Marquetly. Activation is when someone takes the first step with your product toward having a great experience. For Marquetly, that would be taking the assessment so that they understand which courses to take. Activating people well at the beginning leads to retention down the line.

Now not every company has the same path to monetizing users. This path works for consumer products with a *freemium* attribute. If you are a B2B product with a sales team, you generate revenue before users have activation. You can swap the order of these to match your product's flow.

With the right funnel, you can easily calculate the conversion through each step. This informs you as to where people are tending to fall off and allows you to act to fix it. Understanding how many people are in each phase of the funnel also lets you target those cohorts and figure out how to move them into the next one. The goal here is to keep people retained and paying.

Although Pirate Metrics became very popular, some people saw the flaw that it did not talk about user satisfaction. Kerry Rodden, a Googler, created the HEART metrics to account for this.

The HEART Framework

HEART metrics measure *happiness, engagement, adoption, retention,* and *task success.* These are usually used to talk about a specific product or feature. Here, adoption is similar to activation in Pirate Metrics because you are talking about someone using the product for the first time. Retention is the same as in Pirate Metrics.

With HEART, you add in other metrics to talk about how the user interacts with the product. Happiness is a measure of how satisfied the user is with the product. Engagement is a measure of how often users interact with the product. Task success measures how easy it is for a user to accomplish what they were meant to with the product.

You can learn more about HEART metrics in Rodden's article, "How to Choose the Right UX Metrics for Your Product."[1]

---

1 Kerry Rodden, "How to choose the right UX metrics for your product," Medium.com. *http://bit.ly/ 2D77HAi.*

Setting Direction with Data

As I mentioned before, all product-related activities contribute to revenue or cost, at the end of the day, for the business. This is how we connect product metrics to business outcomes. But it's important to have metrics at every level of strategy, including the product initiative and option, so we can tell whether we are successful along the way.

Whatever your metric, it's important to have a system of metrics, not just one, to guide product decisions. It's easy to game one metric when it's your singular focus. Marquetly could have easily fallen into this trap, as well. Whatever options it explores to increase acquisition, it should be sure to keep watching the retention rate of those users and should make sure it doesn't fall below a certain threshold. I call the system of two metrics that balance out each other *mutually destructive pairs*, although there can be more than just two.

There is one issue with this system, though. Retention is a lagging indicator, which is impossible to act on immediately. It will be months before you have solid data to show that people stayed with you. That is why we also need to measure leading indicators like activation, happiness, and engagement. Leading indicators tell us whether we're on our way to achieving those lagging indicators like retention. To determine the leading indicators for retention, you can qualify what keeps people retained—for example, happiness and usage of the product.

Usually, the success metrics we set around options are leading indicators of outcomes we expect on our initiatives, because options are strategies on a shorter time scale, as we talked about in the previous chapter. The success metrics need to be commensurate with the length of the bet there. Measuring the metrics at your option level helps to prevent surprises when the cold, hard facts come in later at the initiative level.

To make sure you have enough data to act on, it's important to implement tools that make it easy to measure these things. This is one of the first things every company should do—implement a metrics platform. Amplitude, Pendo.io, Mixpanel, Intercom, and Google Analytics are all data platforms. Some, like Intercom and Pendo.io, also implement good customer feedback loops, because they provide tools to reach out to customers and ask questions. Having a metrics platform implemented, whether it's homegrown or third party, is essential for a product-led company because it enables product managers to make well-informed decisions.

When setting goals, it's important to be realistic. Christa and Karen looked at the survey results and product analytics to help approximate what those numbers might be to make an educated hypothesis. They also looked at historical trends and tried to base their estimates in reality. For example, they knew that they weren't going to acquire over 80,000 new users a month. But they could potentially double their existing acquisition rate because there was so much feedback pointing to lack of applicable content as the problem.

You won't be able to set success metrics without investigating the problem. This is why we first need problem exploration, a process we explain in the next chapter. The success metrics you set will be relevant to that problem you discover and the solution you implement to solve it.

17

Problem Exploration

Christa was leading her team through the Product Kata to kick off their work on exploring the option.

"What is our option's goal?" she asked Matt and Rich.

"Increase the rate of published courses to 50% and increase the number of second courses created by teachers to 30%," they responded.

"Where are we now?"

"We're still at the beginning: the publish rate of those courses that started is only 25%. Pretty dismal. The number of second courses is at just 10%. We're doing *super* well," he snarked. They were all a bit shocked when the data came in, and the feeling was still lingering.

"What is the obstacle standing in our way that we want to tackle?"

"We don't understand enough about the problems the teachers are facing when creating courses."

"What is one step we can take to better understand this?"

"User research," said Matt. "I will line up 20 of our teachers for one-hour sessions and watch them create courses. In two weeks, I should have enough for us to identify the key pain points. Can you help me with the interviewing, Christa?"

"Of course, let's divide and conquer. Rich, can you sit in on a few so we can all be on the same page?"

"Sure, I can come to about half of them this week. I'll clear my schedule."

There was so much angst in those sessions, but it was well warranted. The team video chatted with most of the users and had them screen share. They had a few teachers who hadn't launched their courses yet, and they were able to show them where they were stuck. After the interviews, they synthesized the data and regrouped.

"Wow, the design of this teacher portal is pretty bad. I knew it wasn't good, but this is worse than I thought," said Matt. "The original designers set it up like they were developers." Matt was new to the company and had joined only a month before.

"Well, yeah, because *I* had to design it," sighed Rich. "And I *am* a developer. We had no UX designers until six months ago!"

"Well, in that case you did the best you could," said Matt, trying to save face with a clearly annoyed Rich. "At least we know what the issues are now."

"I had no idea that they also had courses in other systems that they wanted to transfer. I thought they made them all from scratch," said Rich. "I also didn't know how much they work outside the system to create the content. They just want a way to quickly enter it all in."

"I know. This workflow is just completely off. Okay," said Matt. "Let's write out the problems and map out the desired flow for the user, and we can work from there."

"Great. I have a few things that stood out to me. Here's a few problem statements that I was working through as we were interviewing people," said Christa. She showed the team her list:

- When I am transferring my course from another school, I want to easily and accurately upload all my information into Marquetly so that I do not have to spend time reentering everything.
- When I am creating a new course, I want to import all of my content easily so that I can launch faster.
- When I am creating a course, I want an audio-only option so that I can save time creating videos and can appeal to people who like podcasts.
- When I am launching a course, I would like recommendations on pricing so that I can save time researching similar courses.
- When I am creating a course, I want to know what my potential students want to learn so I can create relevant content for them.

"Those look like everything to me," agreed Matt and Rich. "Let's map out our current user journey and identify which areas are bad, and then we can do an ideal state."

They drew the current user journey on the whiteboard and marked the areas that were particularly troublesome.

"I think our biggest opportunity is around solving the time it takes for people to get their content into the system," said Christa. "We should start with that as our problem and then experiment around it."

They wrote down their hypothesis:

We believe that, by helping teachers get their lesson content into the system painlessly and quickly, we can increase the rate of published courses to 50% and increase the number of second courses created to 30%.

Understanding the Problem

Product managers are often spoken about as the "voice of the customer," yet too many of us are not getting out and talking to customers as much as we should. Why? Because it involves talking to (gasp) *people*. It takes a lot of effort to line up the interviews, and sometimes that can seem more daunting than staying inside and jumping right into A/B testing or sifting through data. Although data analysis is important, it can't tell the entire story. So it's essential that we all go talk to actual humans to get to the heart of their problems. In fact, Giff Constable wrote an entire book, called *Talking to Humans*, that can walk you through how to do just that.

User research, observations, surveys, and customer feedback are all tools that you can harness to better explore the problem from a user standpoint. User research, in this case, is not to be mistaken for *usability testing*, which involves showing a prototype or website and directing people to complete actions. There, you are learning whether they can use and navigate the solution easily, not whether the solution actually solves a problem. This type of research is called *evaluative*.

Problem-based user research is *generative research*, meaning that its purpose is to find the problem you want to solve. It involves going to the source of the customer's problem and understanding the context around it. This is what Marquetly did. The team went to the customers, conducted observations, and then asked questions. "What is the biggest problem standing in the way of you finishing your course? What's the pain?" When conducting problem-based research, you are trying to identify the pain point and the root cause of the problem. When you understand the context around a customer's problem, you can form a better solution to solve it. Without that, you are just guessing.

It's easy to fall into the trap of solving problems before you find their root causes. We're all prone to problem solve, even if we don't know what the problem is. Our brains love thinking in terms of solutions. However, this can be risky for business. If you don't have an underlying understanding of the problem, you can never deliberately create the right solution. The only way you can end up there is by luck. I'm not saying that this process is easy, but it's the more efficient, effective, and successful way.

One easy slip when you're in this mode is pretending that the problem is the lack of a feature. I have had many conversations like this one with a company:

Me: "What problem are you solving for your users?"

Company: "Our users don't have custom dashboards."

Me: "So...what is your solution?"

Company: "Custom dashboards."

When I ask why the users want customer dashboards, I get responses like this:

They want to easily look at their most important metrics daily so they can see if a build has broken something.

They want to be able to easily communicate to their boss the progress of their last release and only the metrics they are responsible for.

They want to be able to monitor the goals of their product on a daily basis so they can make decisions about next steps.

These are all legitimate problems that some custom dashboards could solve, but the way you build the dashboard would be slightly different in each case. For the first and third use case, we might create a UI with which they can choose certain metrics to monitor and have them update over a time period. In the second, as a user, I would want a reporting functionality I could define for my boss. Maybe you could create a solution that has both, but if someone has only the second problem, you could save yourself some work.

It's easy to become attached to solution ideas. I get stuck, too, even after doing this for so long. When I think of new ideas for our online school, Product Institute, I get excited and want to implement them right away. Just a few months ago, I had this great idea to jump on the bandwagon of the newest fad in Silicon Valley: chatbots. I thought that if we could put a chatbot on our site and program it to respond to questions the way a coach does, our students would go crazy for it. I had started figuring out how we might be able to implement it quickly and test it when, luckily, our product manager, Casey Cancellieri, was wise enough to say, "Melissa, we just don't need this right now. There is no problem this feature is solving." She was right. Even though this might be a good idea (or a really terrible idea) in the future, it wasn't an in-the-moment need. It was a distraction.

My friend Josh Wexler says, "Nobody wants to hear that their baby is ugly." The way around this is to not get too attached. Kill the bad ideas before they take up too much time and energy from the teams and before you get hooked on them. Instead, fall in love with the problem you are solving.

Users Don't Want an App

A few years ago, the founders of a women-in-business community brought me in to advise on an app idea. I got to work trying to assess where they were in the process and which problem they were solving. Where did this idea for an app come from? After some digging and talking to key people, I discovered that the company had launched an entirely different app the year before and had a very successful download rate. More people were coming to the site, and it really was a boon for acquisition.

The company was convinced it would get a lot of customer business from this new app, as well, but no one was able to determine whether the problem they were solving was the right one. The company had rushed into building features for the sake of getting something out the door rather than trying to understand what its customers wanted and needed.

On my first day, I met with the product and leadership teams to dig deeper into their idea for the new app. This time around, they wanted to use a Tinder-like interface to match women up with potential business mentors. The hypothesis was that women needed access to mentors quickly to help with career advice and advancement, and they were willing to connect with other women in their cities to meet that need. The teams put a lot of weight in that hypothesis. But we decided to take a step back and ask the glaring question: "Do women feel comfortable connecting with strangers for mentorship in this manner?"

We tested that assumption. We interviewed many women and pitched the app idea to those who were struggling to find a mentor. The reaction was not great. "Eww, no," was the typical response. These women didn't want strangers as mentors. They had to discuss intimate details of their work relationship, and they felt they needed something in common before they could build a relationship. Many of these women were finding mentors through referrals by people they trusted: friends of their parents, university alumni, sorority events, at work, or at meetups. They didn't want to swipe to find a mentor.

Through this process, the company learned what the customers wanted, as well as what they didn't want, and that process was revealing. They quickly realized that it wasn't actually building the right thing for its customers. The solution had been invalidated, but they still did not understand whether they were solving the right problem. Following this revelation, I worked with the team to begin looking in more depth at a few of these women's problems around mentorship and business networking, by doing proper problem research through interviews.

After this experience, the team was able to see that, if it tested the hypothesis early, through research and more experiments, it could save a lot of money in the future. The team was already paying a product developer a ton of money to start creating the app, when it could have used a different approach to prove or disprove its desirability in a week. By getting into the mindset of solving problems early, you allow much more time to build the right thing, because you're not wasting time chasing after the wrong things.

Breaking Down Barriers and Getting Creative

In many companies, it's difficult—or even impossible—to talk to the customer, usually due to corporate bureaucracy. In these situations, you need to get creative. A friend of mine, Chris Matts, is a master of navigating company constraints. He once told me about how he was working at a company and was told he could not talk to the customers. He went to the person who set the rule, who then sent him to another person who had apparently set the rule. He kept going up and up the chain until finally getting to the person who really had issued the edict. This person looked at him and said, "What? I never said people couldn't talk to those customers. I just said you had to go through a specific process to do it. Just fill out this form." The next day, he was talking to customers.

Learning some information is better than none. In a consumer industry, you can usually reach out to friends of friends who use the product or have the right background. In a B2B environment, you can work with the sales or account managers to have them be your research spies—asking the questions you might need to know during their sales calls or follow-up meetings. It's not always possible, but in many places, when you think outside the box, you can come up with *something* that helps. In the situation with Marquetly, when it couldn't get in touch with the users who were dropping off before signing up, it turned to Qualaroo.

Even if you have access to the people you need, customer research is not without its pitfalls. It can be tricky because, as you might have experienced already, people often immediately jump into telling you the solution. "Oh, I just need a button here that lets me do X," they say. As a product manager, you need to back up and ask, "Okay, but why? Why do you need a button? Why do you think a button is the right thing? What are you trying to accomplish?" It is understanding the user's need—not the button—that helps you to get closer to understanding the root of the problem.

Remember, it's not the customer's job to solve their own problems. It's your job to ask them the right questions.

Validating the Problem

Back at Marquetly, Christa and her team were getting a real-life lesson in problem validation.

"So we're betting that, if we make it painless and quick to get content into the system, we can increase the number of published courses. What if we just automated the creation of the course? They could easily upload all their content somewhere, and we could just take care of putting into the right place," Christa proposed.

"Hmm, that could be interesting, but I think there's a bunch of nuances with it," said Rich. "For example, are the things they are entering all standardized? There would be so many different fields, and every course isn't technically the same. We wouldn't be able to do that unless they followed a specific format for the course—like if everyone had a video, caption, block of text, etc. I'm a bit skeptical."

Christa thought about it for a moment. "I think you're right, but I just don't know. Maybe they want more control over the content, maybe they don't," she said. "Why don't we run a small test to see whether we understand if they want to customize their types of content or if they were okay following a certain format? Maybe they are experts on course design and are particular about it, or maybe they're looking to us for guidance."

I was sitting there observing. They were on the right path, but they needed to really frame out what they wanted to learn. "Let's go back to the Kata and walk through it," I said. "What did you learn on your last step?"

"We learned more about the teachers' problems. We know that they have trouble getting the content into the system. Figuring out how our system works seems to be the biggest hurdle."

"Great," I said. "Now what is your current state, based on that last step?"

"We are still where we were in relation to the goal. We haven't moved any closer to it."

"Okay, so what is the biggest obstacle standing in the way of your reaching that goal?" I asked the team. "What do you need to learn next?"

Christa was quiet for a minute and then chimed in, "The next thing we need to learn in order to move forward is how to solve the biggest pain point for the user—getting the content into the system—and what about that is taking so long. We don't know how they want the content to appear or whether they are picky about format. We don't know if they would follow a template, which would be easier for us, or if they want control."

"It sounds to me like you need to do some generative solution research," I said. "That means you need to answer questions like, 'What do they value in a solution?' This is less about proving a hypothesis and more about understanding what would make a good solution to test."

"We can reach out to five teachers who were starting new courses and offer them a *service* to get all their content in the system," Rich said. "We'll just take on the work and do it ourselves. We can see what types of things they submit. We can even try testing around a template and see whether we can get them to give it to us in a certain format."

"I like that," said Christa. "Let's start without the template first so we can see what should go in it. We can take five teachers and allow them to submit their content in any form they want and see what types of things they submit."

"Sounds like you are on the right track," I said. "When can I come back and see what you have learned?"

"It should take us about two weeks to finish this, so let's regroup then," Christa said. The team was off to run their experiment.

They reached out to 20 teachers who had just begun creating a new course and asked them if they were having trouble getting their course into the system. Ten answered yes, and they pitched their service as, "We'll take on the work to get your course into the system—you just have to get us the content. Then you can take a look and edit whatever you would like." Five teachers agreed to work with them over the next two weeks.

They asked the teachers to send them whatever they had in any format that worked for them. Things came in to them in all shapes and forms. There were Dropbox links, Google Docs, spreadsheets of curriculum, and links to YouTube. The most surprising thing was the format the videos came in. Teachers were sending them unedited, with instructions on how they wanted them edited. The audio files came separately.

"I didn't think we were going to be video editing for them," Christa was saying. "I thought we told them they had to send us finished content."

Rich was just as perplexed. "I don't know what to do with this. I'm not a video editor. I thought they were having trouble getting things into our system, not creating the materials themselves."

Matt had spent extensive time with the users and thought he understood what was going on. "Remember, they aren't experts in creating online courses. They are good at developing curriculums but not necessarily at making videos. What if we understood the problem wrong? What if it isn't getting the content into the system but creating online content—videos in particular—that is the problem?"

The team members stared at one another. "We have to follow up with these teachers. Let's dive in more." They went out to talk with the teachers and heard the same story over and over again. "Your website sucks and it's pretty hard to get things into the system, but that isn't my biggest problem. It takes me so long to create a course because I have to learn how to edit videos and create videos that are engaging. If I could create videos faster, I would be able to finish this course in half the time."

"Wow," Rich said. "We completely missed the real problem. We have to redesign that flow one day, but the bigger problem here is creating videos. I wonder how much that scales."

The team conducted a survey with all of its teachers and found that, by far, video creation was one of the biggest pain points the teachers had. They were spending upward of two months editing the videos. Most teachers who did not finish publishing the course said it was the result of too much time spent trying to create and edit videos. One user said, "I know how to film the videos technically, but trying to figure out what makes a good video and then editing it is beyond me." Another even said, "I spent four days trying to shoot one video last week because I kept screwing up my script in the middle."

"I think we just found our real problem," said Rich.

18

Solution Exploration

I met with the team again two weeks later to review what it learned.

"We found a bigger problem standing in the way of reaching our goal," said Christa, grinning. "Our teachers are spending upward of 80 hours over two months editing videos for their class. There are some people who are even reshooting the videos over and over again so they don't have to edit."

I was very proud of them. "See, trying to solve one problem uncovered a bigger one. What is the next step?" I asked.

"We're running an experiment to see whether taking on video editing for a select group of our teachers will result in more courses being published from that group," said Christa. The team began to walk through the Kata to determine what it needed to learn next.

"We know that video editing is a problem for most of our teachers, but we need to learn whether solving this problem will increase the published rate of courses," said Rich.

"Perfect," I said. "Now how do you make that happen?"

The team scoped out its experiment. They would pitch the video-editing service to the teachers and help up to 10 of them per week for two weeks. There were two video editors at Marquetly working in its marketing department. Christa asked Karen to get buy-in from the VP of marketing to have them help execute on the experiment for two weeks, and he agreed. Together, they determined that they could handle about seven courses per week together, in that amount of time.

With that in mind, and already knowing the potential revenue each published course could bring in, Christa set their success metric to be at least 10 of the courses they worked on to be published within a month.

Two weeks after launching the experiment, I came back to check on the team and see what it learned.

"Well, it didn't go as we expected, but we learned things. For example, we found that most teachers have no idea what *good* videos even look like for an online class. So, we ended up advising them on how to make their videos entertaining," said Christa.

"Based on that," Rich continued, "we are thinking that a good solution will include a guide on making videos or maybe some kind of template."

"We saw very good results, and we'd like to keep going, but I don't think this experiment will scale to more than 14 people every two weeks" said Christa.

"Well, that's to be expected," I replied. "The type of experiment you are running is a concierge experiment. They are, by nature, expensive because you're manually taking on the work. You need to learn what makes sense in the solution and then think about how you can scale this to a sustainable offering—that is, if it proves your hypothesis. This is great work. Let's check back in and see whether the teachers give the green light to publish within the month."

The team went back to work and started identifying the solution components that mattered to its teachers:

- Recipe or how-to guide for successful video creation
- Ability to splice together talking-head video, slides, images, audio, and YouTube videos
- Ability to show text on top of the video
- Introduction slide to the video

They also thought about what type of experience or factors would make or break the solution:

- Control over the finished product
- Ease of getting information to the editors
- Human language on what is needed—not technical speak

While the team was thinking through how these factors might turn into a scalable offering, they started to see courses go live. Within one week after the videos were edited and uploaded to the site, half of the teachers whom the team had assisted had published their courses. By the end of three weeks, 12 teachers had published. Success!

Experimenting to Learn

The Marquetly team understood that there was a lot of uncertainty around the problem it was trying to tackle. Video editing was not a core value proposition for the organization, so it had to deeply understand the requirements from a user perspective in order to figure out how to solve it in a scalable way that made sense for the company. This is why experimenting to learn was key.

Companies often confuse the *building to learn* and *building to earn*. Experimentation is all about building to learn. It allows you to understand your customers better and to prove whether there is value in solving a problem. Experiments should not be designed to last for a long time. By nature, they are meant to prove whether a hypothesis is true or false, and, in software, we want to do this as quickly as possible. This means you'll need to eventually scrap whatever you build and figure out how to make it sustainable and scalable, if it does succeed.

Since *The Lean Startup* was published, companies have been adopting experimentation techniques, yet many of them have done so for the wrong reasons. They all are trying to build the ideal Minimum Viable Product (MVP), an experimentation concept introduced in the book. I asked my Twitter followers how they defined an MVP at their company. A bunch of people replied, but one follower summed it up well: "I was told by two separate clients that whatever is built in the first release is an MVP."

This type of thinking is exactly what lands us in the build trap. When we use an MVP only to get a feature out quicker, we're usually cutting corners on a great experience in the process. Thus, we sacrifice the amount we can learn from it. The most important piece of the MVP is the learning, which is why my definition has always been "the minimum amount of effort to learn." This keeps us anchored on outcomes rather than outputs.

Due to the misconception of this term, I have stopped using MVP altogether. Instead, I talk more about solution experimentation. These experiments are designed to help companies learn faster. Here we are experimenting to learn, not building to earn. We are not creating stable, robust, and scalable products. Often, we don't know what the best solution would even be when we begin experimenting. That is the point in doing this work.

The Product Kata is a great tool for grounding people in learning. It always asks the question, "What do you need to learn next?" This keeps the team on track and sets it up to create the right type of experiments.

There are many ways to experiment to learn. Concierge, Wizard of Oz, and concept testing are three examples of solution experiments, each of which I explain shortly.

Because these are not designed to be long-lasting solutions, you want to limit exposure to your customers. With any experiment, it is important to think of how you will end it—to "close the loop." Setting expectations on experiments with your customers is key to keeping them happy and to mitigating risk of a failed experiment. Explain to them why you are testing, when and how the experiment will end, and what you plan to do next. Communication is key to a successful experimentation process.

CONCIERGE

The experiment that Marquetly ran with its teachers is called a *concierge* experiment. Concierge experiments deliver the end result to your client manually, but they do not look like the final solution at all. Your customers will understand that you're doing it manually and that it's not automated. It's one of my favorite experiment types because it doesn't involve coding and it's quick to get started. Because you get to work with your customers closely, there is a ton of feedback flowing through and there are tight learning loops.

Concierge experiments are particularly interesting for B2B companies because this is how many of these companies got started—by taking on the work for the customers and then later automating it. By taking on the work yourself, you can learn how to build the software correctly the first time. And it's far faster and less expensive to iterate on a service than on a coded feature. I frequently used this type of experiment to learn about my customers when I worked as a product manager.

At an SEO company, we used Excel to model a forecasting tool to predict where organizations' keywords would rank. We were able to deliver the spreadsheet manually to a few clients and gauge their response. We learned what types of factors they were most interested in controlling and what percentage of certainty made them feel comfortable. After a month of using spreadsheets, we were able to code the feature into our product and to launch to our user base with wide success.

Concierge experimenting can be a very powerful tool. The thing to note with this method is that it does not scale, given that it's labor intensive. You should conduct these experiments with just enough users so that you can stay in regular contact with them, get plenty of feedback, and then use that information to iterate. As Marquetly did, you can calculate how many people you can handle over a certain period of time. When you are ready to see whether your solution scales to more people, you should use another type of experiment.

WIZARD OF OZ

The method I suggest for reaching a broader audience for feedback is called the Wizard of Oz. The idea behind the Wizard of Oz is that, unlike the concierge experiment, it looks and feels like a real, finished product. Customers don't know that, on the backend, it's all manual. Someone is pulling the strings—just like the Wizard of Oz.

Zappos actually started with this Wizard of Oz method. Back in the day, founder Nick Swinmurn wanted to see whether people would really buy shoes online. He put a simple website up on WordPress. Visitors could view and then buy the shoes online. But, on the backend, it was just Nick, singlehandedly running around, buying shoes from Sears and shipping them out from UPS himself, as each order came in. There was no infrastructure, no inventory of shoes, no person manning the phones. It was simply a page where the founder waited for orders. As soon as the orders came in, he went and fulfilled them. Through this approach, he validated that there was demand for buying shoes online without building out the entire site. That's the Wizard of Oz method.

This is a great technique, when you are looking for feedback at scale. We used this to prove a hypothesis around subscriptions at an e-commerce company where I worked. The head of operations had a great idea on how to sell more of our existing products. This was right around the time when Amazon implemented its one-click subscription services, and he saw that it could apply to us, as well. We had many products on our site that required people to reorder them every month—protein powder, vitamins, and supplements, for example.

He came to me with the idea and asked us to explore how much effort it would be to implement. Unfortunately, our third-party shipping management system did not support subscription-based products, and it would have been a significant development haul. We calculated out roughly how much it would cost to do it completely and designed a Wizard of Oz experiment to see whether the subscriptions would bring in enough revenue to justify the effort.

We then ended up just duplicating every product that qualified for a subscription, renamed it with "subscription" attached to the title, and added in a simple PDF agreement at checkout. It looked like a normal subscription product to the customers, but, on the back end, the customer service team would pull the orders on those products and reorder it for people every month. We kept track of those sales for four months and found that many people would cancel their subscriptions in the second or third month. That was strange. I mean, if they wanted to keep using the product, they would need to reorder it.

I called some of the people to find out. There was one common problem. They said, "I want to feel like I have control over my purchases. I subscribe to too many things now. I would rather reorder on my own." Knowing this, we tried a different approach. We ended up sending a simple email every month to those people buying products that needed to be reordered. Sales skyrocketed! And, because we experimented first, we ended up saving over $100,000 of development costs.

Companies are tempted to leave Wizard of Oz experiments up for a long time because they look real to the customers. This is not wise, because it is still manual on the backend. After you know which direction you want to go in, you can begin to think about the full solution or move on to other forms of experimentation.

Wizard of Oz can also be combined with techniques such as A/B testing. In A/B testing, you split a portion of your traffic to a new solution idea to see whether it moves a metric compared to the current state of the site. You can use this outside of Wizard of Oz, as well, to test new designs or messages on your website.

But you need to be careful about when you use A/B testing. You wouldn't want to use A/B testing in two instances: if you were still very unsure about your solution direction or if you did not have enough traffic to those pages for the results to have statistical significance. If the latter, you could use techniques like concept testing to get feedback.

CONCEPT TESTING

Concept testing is another solution experiment that focuses more on high-touch interaction with the customer. In this case, you try to demonstrate or show concepts to the user to gauge their feedback. These can vary in execution, from landing pages and low-fidelity wireframes to higher-fidelity prototypes or videos of how the service might play out. The idea here is to pitch the solution idea in the fastest, lightest way possible to convey the message.

It's important to note that this type of experiment tends to be more generative than evaluative. Just like problem research, generative solution experiments help you to gain more awareness around what a user desires in a solution. When you show the concept to users, you are asking them to put themselves into the scenario in which they are experiencing the problem, and you are asking them questions about how the solution would or would not solve their problem.

If you want to make it evaluative, to firmly test a hypothesis, you need a definitive pass-or-fail criteria, when interviewing a customer about the concept. This can be what I call an *ask*—something you would need from the user, either in the form of a commitment, monetary value, time, or some other investment that shows they are interested. Landing pages almost always pitch the idea and contain an ask in the form of entering an email address.

In many early-stage companies, concept testing is the way they get early sales or capital. This is how Dropbox got its first round of investment.[1] When starting out, Dropbox had the hunch that the biggest issue it could solve for users was seamless synchronization of their documents across computers and the internet. The issue was definitely rampant, but the company had a difficult time pitching the solution to investors. When it explained how Dropbox worked, the investors dismissed it, citing a crowded market of similar tools. No matter how hard they tried to explain the solution, the investors just couldn't picture it.

So, the company turned to a solution experiment. The team put together a rough video, demonstrating what Dropbox could do. It had not built a demo or a prototype but instead used video editing to demonstrate what it would look and feel like to the investors. It felt like a real product demo, even though it wasn't a finished product. When the investors saw it, they went wild. To them, it was magic. Dropbox was able to secure it funding and to validate that it was on the right path.

When You Don't Need to Experiment Robustly

At a workshop recently, a product manager asked me, "Do we always need to run these experiments? What if it's an easy problem to fix?" The answer is no. Although concierge, Wizard of Oz, and concept testing are all good techniques, sometimes you don't need to experiment so heavily around multiple concepts. It is important to remember that these tools are used for higher amounts of uncertainty and, thus, larger risk in your solution ideas.

For example, I worked with one team that was experimenting around how to reduce the amount of calls to a help desk at its office. The team found an issue where an expected button was not being displayed on the screen. Being excellent students of this methodology, they wanted to deploy an A/B test, displaying the button for half of the participants and measuring the change. I told the team that wasn't the right approach. In this case, the team knew the problem and the solution. It was time to implement it. There was no need for up-front testing, but they should still be measuring whether it reduces calls after the implementation.

1 "How DropBox Started as a Minimal Viable Product," TechCrunch. *https://tcrn.ch/2Pnolfp*.

Often, the solution is not as cut and dried as the missing button but not as nebulous as some of the other examples we've gone over in this chapter. In this case, you should still be building to learn instead of rushing into a complete solution, but there are other tools you can harness, such as prototypes.

Prototypes are the most popular tool for testing. When you need to learn whether a specific user flow or feature solves a problem for the user and allows them to achieve their desired outcome, you can turn to prototypes. It is an excellent tool because prototypes don't require any code, and there are many software products out there that can help you link screens together to make the flow feel real.

But, if you don't go the design sprint route when creating your prototype, which includes heavy user research before diving into design, you can easily become stuck trying to solve a problem you don't yet understand. Prototypes don't make sense when you need to validate the problem. In this case, you're spinning your wheels creating shiny designs that look great but don't help you to learn what you need to learn. That's why you need to focus on exploring the problem before any solution activities.

It's important to remember that any experiment type must be used appropriately and in the right context. That said, you also can and should use your own creativity to come up with different types of experiments to help clarify the questions you need to answer before you converge on the solution idea. Get creative! Just remember that your biggest objective in this phase is to learn—not to earn.

Experimenting in Complex Industries

When I introduce the concept of experimenting to learn, I am frequently met by the same response: "That sounds nice, but we just can't do that here." That's just wrong.

Of course, not every industry can take advantage of landing pages or Wizard of Oz, because they are best suited for consumer products. But these are only two types of experiments. If a good experiment helps you learn, you can always find a way within your constraints. Making known the unknown reduces risk, and that goes for large, bureaucratic companies like banks, as well as for industries with long product development timelines, like aviation. There is no excuse for not learning.

Even the most seemingly Waterfall projects can be experimental. Consider developing a space shuttle. Even though it takes years to build this complex system, and it involves hardware, there are still possible experiments along the way.

For example, testing the panels to see whether they will withstand the heat of an engine is an experiment. You hypothesize, test, and then iterate to find the right material combination. After it is known, it gets built as a component of the space shuttle. This is how we should be approaching products in any industry.

In 2014, I advised a company in London called GiveVision, while I was mentoring startups at the Wayra accelerator. The GiveVision mission was to help sight-impaired people "see" by providing glasses that would read, recognize, and report on what was going on in the world around them. After I got over my feelings of, "These people are literally saving the world. What the hell am I doing with my life?" we sat down to talk about the company's product development process. I learned that the development timeline for its glasses would be on the order of years. The organization had to program the software with a third-party manufacturer and couldn't iterate on it afterward because it was hardcoded into the glasses and couldn't be updated after it was installed. I talked to founders about the concept of risk and how the company might mitigate it with experimentation. The founder said that the biggest risk was that there were so many options for what could be programmed into the glasses and no one was sure which ones were the highest value items. That's when the company decided to experiment.

When I came back a month later, I was astounded by the progress the group had made. To learn what its potential users cared about the most, the company had done a few things. First, it did a lot research which included following and observing how sight-impaired people go about their day. Team members learned about their customers' biggest frustrations, how they might position themselves around certain obstacles, and what type of information they were seeking.

One woman said, "Every day I have to take a certain bus to work, but I can never tell which bus is approaching the stop, so I need to flag down all of them. When I get on, I ask the driver but immediately get off when I know it's the wrong one. As I'm leaving the bus, I can hear everyone sighing that I held them up. I wish I could read the route number of the bus as it approaches."

Stories like this piled up. GiveVision used these anecdotes and observations to identify the most important problems it could solve. The priority became reading signs (like the one identifying the bus number), nutritional information, currency, and colors.

The next question to answer was, "Can we make the software recognize and report in a way that satisfies the user?" This is where it got tricky. To program anything into the glasses, the turnaround time for the manufacturer would be about six months. Because GiveVision couldn't iterate quickly on this timeline, not to mention the cost to produce new glasses every time, the company got creative.

It programmed an Android phone with the software that would run on the glasses using the camera as a lens. To simulate the position and height, engineers used a 3D printer to create "glasses" that the phone strapped into that went over the head. Now they could give the "glasses" to their users to test out and wear around for the day.

I got to try one myself, as you can see in Figure 18-1. Sure, I looked a little silly, but it worked! I could wander around while the technology recognized currency, colors, and signs, and it spoke the information to me through the accompanying headphones. It was awesome. GiveVision's users were excited for the new experience, even if it was clunky. They gave feedback on the type of answers the software used, the positions, the timing, everything. This bit of creativity allowed the company to learn a lot without having to go through months or years of manufacturing.

Figure 18-1. *The GiveVision experiment*

With the risk mitigated on the customer side for the software components, the company could begin programming the glasses. Six months later, it had a prototype of real glasses that went beyond the first experiment, which it used to raise money and simulate more trials.

Learning reduces risk. The goal of solution exploration is to get faster feedback. If we take too long to get feedback, we not only waste money but we also waste time. The opportunity cost of building the wrong thing is too high. Every industry and product has unknowns—getting creative about how you answer these unknowns is key.

Experimenting on Internal Products

I often hear, "Do I *really* have to use these techniques for internal tools?" Yes, absolutely.

My second product management job was overseeing the development of all the internal tools for the e-commerce company I have talked about throughout this book. Actually, I played a dual role as both the product manager and the UX designer. Building that system ended up being a turning point for me in my career. Until that time, I thought that, because customers never saw our internal tools, the experience or design didn't really matter. It was more about getting the functionality out there.

A year of building with that mentality, and I had a pretty rude awakening. I remember one week when I was working from home almost every day; my boss asked me why I wasn't coming into the office. I told him, "I have had lines of people at my desk asking me to upload the products for them because they can't figure out the tools. I need to get work done. I can't be everyone's help desk." He paused for a moment and then looked at me and said, "Well, if they can't figure out how to use the tools, that's on you, not them."

He was right. I was not satisfying my users' problems. Actually, I was making their job more difficult.

I began approaching my work just as any other product manager with external users would. I wrote down their problem statements, did research with them, experimented around offerings, and started to deeply connect with the way they worked. We used concierge experiments, concept testing, and lots of prototyping. I even learned that it was easier to do this work with my users because they were in the same building as me.

When I started working this way, we saw a huge change. Our internal users were happier, and we reduced the churn of the employees in this position who had previously felt handicapped to do their job well. These people were also able to get more done, and the operating costs for our business went down as a result of not having to keep hiring at an incredible pace.

Internal tools are often neglected, but they still matter to the company. They need to be treated the same way as any other product. You need to understand the direction, diagnose the problem, learn more about it, and then learn what the right solution is. After you have experimented to prove value, you can concentrate on building your first version and optimizing.

Choosing the Right Solution at Marquetly

After the team validated that video editing was the issue, it was time for Karen to step in as the VP of product and evaluate their options. Given that a considerable amount of investment would be needed, she had to present the case to the leadership team for buy-in. I was discussing the options with her.

"This is a build, partner, or buy decision," she told me. "We can either build a service, by hiring video editors full time or freelance. We could build software that does video editing ourselves. Or, lastly, we can buy a video-editing technology that is user-friendly and embed it into our teacher platform. The last one is the best, margin-wise, but there is risk that the teachers won't be able to use it. I have to research what is out there."

Karen went away to explore different video-editing software that had the elements of a solution Christa's team had discovered during its experiment. She found a company out of Budapest that did exactly what they were looking for—find and add background music, easily splice together videos, sync up separate audio tracks, and write text over the video. All of that, in a simple-to-use interface. But there was still risk on the user side. She went to Christa to plan their next experiment.

"We need to learn whether the users can even use this software to edit on their own. We did all the work for them last time," Karen explained to Christa. "Can you run another experiment, where you have the users try the video-editing software from the company in Budapest and see whether they can navigate it?"

"Yeah, that sounds like a plan. Okay, we'll do another round of testing, similar to the first time, and measure whether people use the video software, and, if so, publish their courses within the month."

The team onboarded 40 teachers into their experiment—a mix of new teachers and ones who had previously published well-received courses. They gave them a 30-minute rundown on how to use the video-editing software, along with a guide on how to make great videos. Then they left them to it and asked them to reach out if they had questions.

Some questions began trickling in that first week, but they were nothing the team couldn't handle. A lot of the confusion was around a slightly complicated user experience in the software, but, with minimal help, the teachers were able to navigate it. The team made a note that, if it did acquire the software, it would need to redesign some elements of the interface.

After three weeks, the team began to see the courses being posted. By the end of the month, 30 of the 40 teachers had published their courses. It wasn't quite as high of a publish rate as the concierge experiment, but it was far more than the 25% publish rate that was normal for teachers without the video-editing software. They deemed the experiment a success, and Karen was able to use the data from the Product Kata, as shown in Table 18-1, to pull together its business case to bring to the senior leadership team.

Table 18-1. *The Product Kata for Marquetly's team*

Current state	What to learn?	Next step	Expected	Learned
Published course rate is 25% and second course rate is 10%.	What problems the teachers are facing when creating courses?	User research: 20 teachers	Understand the biggest problems.	Trouble transferring courses, importing content, audio options, pricing recommendations.
Published course rate is 25% and second course rate is 10%.	What is the biggest pain point for getting content into the system?	Work with 20 teachers to upload content into the system.	Come away with top issues that are taking the teachers the longest.	Video editing is taking teachers too long.
Published course rate is 25% and second course rate is 10%.	Do most teachers have a problem with video editing?	Survey to test for scale.	Out of 100 teachers, most have issues with video editing.	90% of teachers say video editing is their biggest hurdle, upwards of 2 months of time spent.
Published course rate is 25% and second course rate is 10%.	Will taking away the video-editing work for teachers cause them to launch their school?	Concierge experiment: conduct video editing for them.	Out of 14 teachers, 10 courses will be published within a month.	12 teachers had published by end of the month, needed guidance on creating good videos.
Published course rate is 75% for experiement, still 25% for general population.	Will teachers use a video-editing software successfully so we can scale?	Onboard 40 teachers to software from company in Budapest.	20 out of the 40 teachers publish within a month.	30 out of the 40 teachers published within a month.

19

Building and Optimizing Your Solution

"As you know, one of our strategic intents is to double revenue growth from our individual users in two years," Karen was saying to the leadership team at Marquetly. "We believe that by increasing the amount of content on our site in key areas of interest, we can double acquisition and increase our retention of existing users to 70%, resulting in a potential revenue increase of $8 million a year from individual users. Christa's team found a big issue in getting more content on our site. Only 25% of teachers who started a course actually published one to our site, and only 10% of our teachers publish a second course."

"WHAT?! That is insane. I had no idea those were the numbers. That's terrible," Chris, the CEO, exclaimed.

"Yeah, it's pretty dismal," Karen agreed. "The major cause is video editing. Our teachers are experts in marketing—not in video editing. They are spending upward of 80 hours trying to just edit videos. We ran two small experiments over the last month to help solve this problem, and we were able to increase the publish rate from 25% to 75%, by providing our teachers with simple-to-use video-editing software. We're also seeing preliminary trends that say these new courses are reengaging previously checked-out students."

"This is incredibly promising. What do we have to do to make this happen for everyone? Can we just implement what you did for the experiment across all teachers?" asked the CTO.

"From a monetary standpoint, we can't afford to provide licenses to all of our teachers. The ROI is not there. Also, if we were to build the functionality ourselves, it would take us over a year to launch the first version. The software we used is from a company in Budapest, and I'm proposing we acquire them. We could then integrate the technology seamlessly into our platform. If their technology is in good shape, we'd be able to launch a first version in a few months. In the meantime, we could figure out a partnership to help people in the shorter term," Karen finished.

"What are the risks to doing this?" asked the CFO.

"We have eliminated most of the risks," said Karen. "By experimenting first, we were able to determine that the teachers will do video editing on their own if given the right tools, like this software from Budapest, and they will actually publish their courses. So, from a teacher standpoint, we are very certain that this is a problem worth solving and that this solution will work for them. From a business standpoint, I've calculated the cost of acquiring this company and the potential ROI is high. It will take less effort from our development team, and we'll be able to launch sooner to market."

"That makes sense, and this is great work," said Chris. "I want to solve this problem. We'll regroup as a senior leadership team and determine the best way to move forward. In the meantime, let's reach out to the company in Budapest and see if we can work out a partnership to get a bulk license to their product for our teachers to use. If we know this works, we might as well get everyone using it."

Two months later, the Marquetly team had made an offer to the company in Budapest to acquire them, and, a month after that, the deal was done. Christa's team laid out a vision for integrating the video-editing software into the teacher platform.

"Our video-editing software will offer teachers the simplest, fastest way to create engaging videos for their students," Christa was saying to the team. "We allow teachers to splice video content from their own and third-party videos, sync up external audio, find and add background music, and put text overlays on the screen. We also know the teachers will need a guide that helps them understand how to create engaging videos—practical tips and tricks as they go. Then we need a way to seamlessly upload the final video into their course."

Matt created early customer journeys and rapid prototypes to make sure the teachers could understand how to use the platform. He tested them, as the team was integrating the backend of the video software into the Marquetly system. After receiving feedback, the team regrouped to determine where to start. Matt combined Christa's vision with his wireframes into a document that they called their North Star.

The team used a technique called *story mapping*, created by product management veteran and consultant Jeff Patton, to make sure they all understood the work and to prioritize the first release. They then prioritized the work, cutting out a few less-critical components in the first version.

"Okay, it looks like we have our work for the first version," said Rich. "With the work we've done to integrate the systems, we should be able to get this out in a month."

"Yes, and I've been calculating success criteria on this first version. This is what I have:

- "Adopted by 75% of our teachers currently creating or starting courses within one month."
- "Published course rate increases from 25% to at least 60%."
- "Time to create a new course decreases from three months to less than one month."

"Rich, can you make sure we can measure these things for the first release?" asked Christa.

"Sure," Rich responded. "We'll make sure analytics are set up so we can keep tracking these things as we go."

"Great," said Christa. "I'll work with the teacher-outreach and marketing teams to create communication on how we will inform our teachers and train them in the new product."

As the team built the functionality, Matt would test screens with a few select teachers to make sure they could navigate it with their own content. They iterated along the way, until the day came for the first release.

Feeling confident, the team launched its new video-editing capabilities to the teachers and waited to see how they were received. Within one week, they could see the adoption of the features begin to increase. They reached out to the teachers periodically to see how they were receiving the new capabilities. There were a few issues that they prioritized in the next release, but things seemed to be going smoothly.

After a month, Christa pulled the numbers to compare to the team's success metrics. "Our adoption rate isn't quite where we need it to be," she told the team. "We only had 60% of the teachers adopt the video-editing software in that first month. The ones who did adopt it are surpassing our previous published course rate with a 75% publish rate. We need to figure out what is standing in the teachers' way of taking us up on it. Let's reach out to those who did not adopt it last month and find out why."

I walked over to Christa to talk to her after the team left. "I love that you're still diagnosing the problems, like the Product Kata taught you."

"This is how I think now!" she said. "I don't even need the board. I'm just always looking for that problem and what I need to learn."

"That's exactly what it's designed to do," I smiled. "I'm so excited to see how far this team has come. Keep doing what you're doing."

The team worked to keep iterating on its new video-editing functionality until it reached its goals. After a few months, the results were speaking for themselves. A 75% publish rate, happier teachers, and an increased number of published second courses all spoke to the success.

Evolving the Product Vision

Christa's team was able to find a scalable, successful solution by iterating its way to a product vision. As I mentioned in the strategy section, it evolved through experimentation. Had the team jumped into dictating features early on, it might never have found the right solution for its customers. The team probably would have still been stuck on redesigning the course creation workflow, which it later proved was not the biggest problem.

After the direction is set for the product vision, it's important to make sure everyone understands the context and work that needs to be done. *Story mapping* and North Star documents are two ways to help teams find alignment around the vision.

A North Star document explains the product in a way that can be visualized by the entire team and company. This includes the problem it is solving, the proposed solution, the solution factors that matter for success, and the outcomes the product will result in.

North Stars are great for providing context to a wide audience. They should be evolved over time, as you learn more about your product. It's important to note that this is not an action plan—it does not include how the team will be building the product. That is where *story mapping* comes in.

Story mapping helps teams break down their work and align around goals. As Patton says, "Its purpose is to help the team communicate about their work and what needs to get done to deliver value." Christa's team used *story mapping* to think through all the factors needed to deliver a successful solution. This included breaking down each desired action from the user standpoint.

Building understanding as a team helps you develop product faster, which means getting value out to the customers faster. You don't want to sacrifice that.

After you have understanding around where you are going, it also makes it easier to scale back to a Version 1 of your product. You need to always start at that big picture—the North Star—to do this well, though. Otherwise, there is nothing to anchor you, and you end up leading yourself into the build trap.

Prioritizing Work

To get to a Version 1, you need to prioritize your work. Prioritization, as I mentioned earlier, is a top issue for most product managers. There are many frameworks out there that will help you prioritize, like *benefits mapping*, *Kano models*, and others, but my favorite is *Cost of Delay*. If you understand the desired outcomes from a strategic perspective, you can use Cost of Delay to help you determine what to ship sooner.

In his book, *The Principles of Product Development Flow*, Don Reinertsen talks about the importance of Cost of Delay in prioritizing work. He calls it "the one thing" that should be quantified. Cost of Delay is a numeric value that describes the impact of time on the outcomes you hope to achieve. It combines urgency and value so that you can measure impact and prioritize what you should be doing first.

When you think of building and releasing that first version of the product, you need to consider the trade-offs between the amount of value you can capture with the scope of the release and the time it takes to get it out the door. It's an optimization problem. You want to reduce scope enough so that you can capture the maximum value in the right time.

If you wait too long because you overscoped the release, you lose the money you could have been making. Worse, a competitor could swoop in and steal your market. Then you'd have a higher threshold to entry, and your product will need to be light years better than the competition's. On the flip side, you don't want to release something that is terrible and provides minimal benefit to the user in order to get it out early. Then you could lose early adopters, and it's difficult to win someone back after they've had a terrible experience.

Christa's team discussed the Cost of Delay involved with shipping the third-party video feature in their first version. It decided that, because it wasn't a critical component for a large number of users, and it would take another month to code that part of the product, the product should not include it. Shipping faster was ideal since every week the company delayed meant a course that wouldn't be published.

You might be thinking, "But how do I calculate the revenue for each of my products?" Ozlem Yuce and Joshua J. Arnold are the experts in Cost of Delay, and they have created a qualitative way to assess it, as illustrated in Figure 19-1.

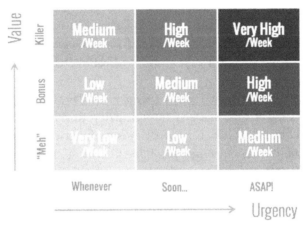

Figure 19-1. *Qualitative cost of delay, by Joshua Arnold and Ozlem Yuce (reprinted by permission of Joshua Arnold and Ozlem Yuce)*

In this situation, you would discuss each feature or feature component in terms of urgency and value. If it is high urgency, that means that every moment you do not ship that feature to customers, you are losing out on opportunity to hit your goal—for example, if you are actively losing customers or revenue each week because you are not fulfilling a need. High value is about solving the strongest problems or desires for the customer.

In Marquetly's case, the features that were highest in urgency and value were adding the audio and splicing the content with images. These were two critical components for their solution and were prioritized first. The rest fell near the higher end of this matrix, except for video splicing. This was only utilized by a few teachers, and great videos could still be created without it. Thus, the urgency and value were a bit lower, and it was not prioritized for the first release.

Cost of Delay can help end many debates about what should and should not be prioritized first. If you want to learn more, head to Black Swan Farming (*http://blackswanfarming.com*) and read about how to utilize the concept in your company.

It's important to remember that, after you ship the first version, though, you are not technically done. You still need to reach your goals. This is where the *Definition of Done* comes into play.

The Real Definition of Done

In Agile development, there is a concept called the Definition of Done. It is defined by the Scrum Alliance as a "checklist of valuable activities required to produce software."[1] When teams create their Definition of Done, it's usually around finishing building features required to ship a product. Although this is definitely a useful concept to make sure the team finished what it needs to, it sets the wrong expectation about what a finished feature is.

We are done developing or iterating on a feature only when it has reached its goals. Often, teams ship a first version of the feature and then move on to the next, without measuring the outcomes for the user. As Jeff Gothelf, the author of *Sense & Respond*, once said, "Version 2 is the biggest lie in software development." This mentality always leads to the build trap.

Instead, teams should be working like the team at Marquetly, by setting the success criteria before launch, while measuring and iterating until they reach it. Version 1 should be looked at as a hypothesis, just like any other work. And, if we launch the feature and it is not hitting our goals, we need to be comfortable rolling it back and trying something else.

When you have success criteria set for the launch, you can use them in the Product Kata and repeat the steps we went through in this section: set the direction with your success criteria, understand what problems are standing in the way of you reaching it, and systematically tackle them through experimentation.

No matter whether you are building a new feature or optimizing one, the process is the same. Problem exploration might be on a shorter time frame if it's around a smaller feature than a new product. The same goes for solution experiments: they might not be as robust as the ones Marquetly was running. But no

---

1 Dhaval Panchal, "What is Definition of Done (DoD)?", *http://bit.ly/2Rjgh2i*.

matter what, you should always be diagnosing the problem and trying to understand how to solve it.

This is how you build with intent and get out of the build trap. But, in addition to having a solid process and strategy, you need a company that supports good product management efforts. Christa's team was able to succeed only because their environment allowed it to. They were able to talk to customers. The team was oriented around outcomes, and then the leadership team gave it the space to figure out how to achieve those outcomes.

These are the marks of a product-led company. Process and frameworks get you only so far on your way to success. Culture, policies, and structure are the things that really set a company apart to thrive in product management.

PART V

The Product-Led Organization

ROLE

STRATEGY

PROCESS

ORGANIZATION

The product-led organization is characterized by a culture that understands and organizes around outcomes over outputs, including a company cadence that revolves around evaluating its strategy in accordance to meeting outcomes. In product-led organizations, people are rewarded for learning and achieving goals. Management encourages product teams to get close to their customers, and product management is seen as a critical function that furthers the business.

"We think the iPhone is going to be big—way bigger than it is now. You should really be looking at how to integrate your camera technology into phones." All nine of our heads bobbed eagerly, as we made our case to the Kodak team. It was 2008, and a big shift in digital photography was in motion. Many of you know what came next for Kodak—it's a well-documented tale of disruption. Well, I was actually there for it and witnessed firsthand what happens when an organization does not plan for innovation.

One year earlier, I had been chosen to participate on an innovation team at Cornell University that was partnering with Kodak Research Laboratories to create a new product that would appeal to people in their early 20s. Kodak Research Laboratories was responsible for researching breakthrough innovations in the area of imaging. Our fearless leaders at Cornell were experimenting with a new way of creating products, in which talking to customers and validating problems preceded any building activity. Kodak was ready for the challenge.

A few months before the project kickoff on January 9, 2007, Steve Jobs had announced the first iPhone. Even though everyone was going absolutely nuts over having the internet on their phone, Kodak was focused on the internet *and* cameras on one device. This was a dangerous combination for its business, as signs were already pointing to disruption. A few years earlier, digital cameras had still been a bit of a novelty. You could tote them around to document every gathering or shenanigan. With the launch of the iPhone, however, we all began leaving our bulky digital cameras at home and using phones as cameras. It was more convenient, and the phones could immediately upload images to Facebook. The market for digital and film-based cameras, core businesses for Kodak, was shrinking.

It was an innovate-or-die situation, and unbeknown to us at the time, my team was at the center of it. Our mission was to find the intersection of what the market really wanted and what Kodak could create. Because we were isolated from the rest of the company, our innovation lab had no roadblocks to prevent us from thinking big. We could fully pursue this mission without worrying about bureaucracy or management shooting down our ideas. But it also kept us in the dark about other areas of Kodak. We were unaware of how, if at all, our work fit into the overall company strategy.

We were targeting people in their late teens and early twenties because they were readily adopting new technology faster than other age groups. Instant messaging and Facebook were leading the charge, and college-aged students were gobbling it all up like Thanksgiving dinner. We saw an opportunity to solve unmet needs, given that these technologies were so new.

Market-driven innovation was the term we coined to explain our process. Over the next few months, we interviewed users in this age group, all while looking for opportunities for Kodak to innovate. We were particularly interested in how our target market balanced real-life interactions with the social capabilities of the new technologies. We organized research groups and held one-on-one conversations to understand the behavioral patterns, the concerns, and the needs. We immersed ourselves in their problems.

Trends began to emerge quickly in our interviews. Although our target user group was generally obsessed with sharing information on Facebook, there was growing concern around who could actually see this information. Technology was rapidly evolving, and the consequences—how that would affect real life— were still unknown. Would employers see my drunken Saturday night where I fell over a parked car? No one knew.

Another need was for controls to enable users to present their best self to the world. "I want to edit my photos and make them look better before I put them online," is something we heard often. People were currently asking their friends who were awesome at Photoshop to edit everything for them. We also heard the pleas for quality images. "I want a better camera on my phone," people would say. "I wish it was the same quality as my digital camera so I could leave that at home."

Between the need for control, photo-editing capabilities, and better camera technology, we felt like we had found the perfect combination of problems to solve for Kodak. It was in their domain, and people were ready for it. Feeling pretty confident about our findings, we presented them to the management team.

"You should really be looking at how to integrate your camera technology into phones," we told them. We went on to explain that the company should explore photo editing. Kodak already had editing software on desktop computers, but we suggested enabling simple photo editing *directly* on the phone itself. We thought that would blow people's minds. Add in the ability to immediately share photos, and you're looking at a huge opportunity. People could geotag their photos with locations, organize them appropriately, and control who could see them.

We then proposed that Kodak move forward in one of two ways—build its own phones and compete with Apple and BlackBerry, or simply provide the technology directly to the already-established phone manufacturers. We left Kodak that day feeling like we had kicked ass. We communicated the opportunity at hand, as well as the level of urgency. It wasn't just about helping Kodak—we actually wanted the products we had pitched. We felt the need for them just as much as the people we interviewed had.

Well, our pitch is a reality now. You can edit photos quickly and easily before you share them with your network. Cell phone cameras are so high tech now that no one uses digital cameras anymore. You can geotag your images, and you have control over who sees what posts. But it wasn't Kodak that built these features. It was Instagram, Apple, Android, and Facebook. So what happened after that meeting?

We heard from Kodak only once before it filed for bankruptcy in 2012. It said it was still looking for a team and budget to pursue the project. I didn't know it at the time, but this was a pattern I would see again and again over the next 10 years in many different companies.

Kodak made good strides in trying to innovate, but its organization prevented it from doing so. The company was reactive rather than strategic, waiting too long to respond to a threat. By isolating a small team in an innovation lab, it also didn't dedicate enough people to thinking about the future of the business.

Even though our team was practicing the discovery process of product management with the right approach, we were in a silo, separated out into an innovation center without the proper resources to fully execute on what we were discovering. Kodak had to secure a new budget to put any of our plans in action, something it couldn't do for another six months during its annual review. Its philosophy as an organization was not set up to succeed in the world of rapid innovation that emerged during the early 2000s.

Many companies are in danger of becoming just like Kodak, but this fate can be avoided by adopting a product-led mindset. Throughout this book, I've laid out what is necessary for a good product management practice. We've talked about the importance of having the right roles with the right people in them and then supporting them with a good product strategy. We then dove deep into how the product management process can uncover the opportunities to achieve that strategy.

However, these processes alone are not enough to get you out of the build trap. As we saw with Kodak, you can be making an effort to understand your customers and to conduct good research, but, without the organization to sustain it, the efforts are too little, too late. To truly get out of the build trap, you need to become a product-led organization, both in mentality and practice. This section dives into those critical components of your organization that you will need to change, such as communication, culture, policies, and rewards.

20

Outcome-Focused Communication

At the next quarterly business review, Karen was able to speak about the accomplishments of the team.

"This quarter, we were able to launch the video-editing software and onboard 150 new classes to our site, all in key areas of interest for our users. Since the launch of those courses, we have seen an increase in acquisition rate from 15% to 25%, and our retention numbers have risen to 60%. We're well on our way to reaching our goals. With the additional efforts fromn other teams around this strategic intent, we'll hit our goal early—within a year and a half."

The senior leadership team was very impressed with the work. A lot had changed in the past year for this company, and it was starting to see the benefits.

A year before, Marquetly was a classic example of a company stuck in the build trap. It was project-oriented, spinning up teams to tackle whatever was prioritized by the CEO. There were no product managers in the organization. Teams never talked to customers and were rewarded for shipping finished software. Those attributes were starting to fade and were being replaced by a customer-centric and outcome-oriented mindset. The company was not finished with its journey of becoming a product-led organization, but it was well on its way. Chris, the CEO, was excited to see the progress.

"It's pretty amazing," he told me, as we caught up after the quarterly business review meeting. "I didn't know what to expect, but I can definitely see progress. We were struggling so much before, and I know there are kinks to work out still, but I'm seeing why this way of working makes sense for us."

"You really are thriving with this," I told Chris. "Many companies do not get to where you are in a transformation like this, but you had the right bones. The senior leadership team—including you—understands outcomes. You get what it means to see results, and you could see the benefits in aligning the strategy through the organization back to them. That is usually where companies get stuck in the build trap. They are not patient enough to see outcomes emerge, so they instead measure progress by the number of features shipped."

"I'm not going to lie," he said. "I was getting a little antsy there, but the meetings to review our progress helped. I think we need to work on having them more frequently, so we have good transparency into the outcomes and activities of the company."

"That's definitely something we can work on," I said. "We can align the cadence so that outcomes are discussed at the right level, for the right people, on a consistent timeline. We'll also get a more standardized roadmap so that everyone can see the progress and what's on deck."

If there is one main reason I have seen companies fail to make a transition, it's the lack of leadership buy-in to move to an outcome-oriented company. Leaders will say that they want to achieve results, but, at the end of the day, they still measure success by features shipped. Why? There's so much satisfaction in seeing things move, at both a leadership and a team level. People want to feel like they are accomplishing things. Checking off the boxes of finished work feels good, but we need to remember that this is not the only measure of success. So we need other ways to help us communicate and talk about progress at different levels.

Without the review meetings, Chris had been antsy because he could not see deeper into what was being done in a way that was meaningful to him. Most executives are just like Chris, so it's important to have a cadence of communication that shows progress at every level of the organization, tailored to each specific audience.

Cadences and Communication

Visibility in organizations is absolutely key. The more leaders can understand where teams are, the more they will step back and let the teams execute. Remember the strategic gaps from Chapter 11? The more you try to hide your progress, the wider that knowledge gap becomes. Leaders will demand more information and will crack down on your freedom to explore. If you keep things transparent, you will have more freedom to become autonomous.

Many companies fall back into bad habits because they have not figured out how to consistently communicate progress across the company in the form of outcomes. When leaders do not see progress toward goals, they quickly resort to their old ways.

We need a cadence of communicating strategy that matches our strategic framework. Remember our four levels of strategy: vision, strategic intent, product initiatives, and options. Each of these is on a different time horizon, and progress toward them should be communicated accordingly.

Most companies I've worked with have a few core meetings to evaluate progress and to make strategic decisions from a product level:

- Quarterly business reviews
- Product initiative reviews
- Release reviews

During *quarterly business review* meetings, the senior leadership team, made up of the executives and the highest level of the organization, should be discussing progress toward the strategic intents and outcomes of a financial nature. This includes reviewing revenue for the quarter, churn of customers, and costs associated with development or operations. The chief product officer (CPO) and their VPs of product are responsible for communicating how the outcomes of product initiatives have furthered strategic intents, like Karen did at Marquetly. New strategic intents can be introduced in this meeting, as older ones are coming to completion. It is not a place to prioritize new product initiatives or to go into detail on them. That is what the product initiative review is for.

The *product initiative review* is another quarterly meeting that can be staggered with the quarterly business review on off months. This meeting is for the product development side of the house—CPO, CTO, design leaders, the VPs of product, and the product managers. Here we review the progress of the options against the product initiatives and adjust our strategy accordingly. This is the place for product managers to talk about the results of preliminary experimentation, research, or first releases, as they relate to overall goals. New product initiatives can be introduced in this meeting for feedback and buy-in, along with funding from the product development leadership group. Product teams can ask for more funding to build a first version or to optimize an existing solution.

Release reviews provide the opportunity for teams to show off the hard work they have done and to talk about success metrics. These should happen monthly, before features go out, to showcase what is in the pipeline to be released. During this meeting, we should be communicating only what we know is going to ship —not experiments or research being conducted. Although not necessary, most executives like to attend this meeting to see what is being shipped out to customers. This can also be a place for teams to communicate their roadmaps internally so that marketing, sales, and the executive team are aware.

It's important to note that not all decisions happen in these meetings. They should be seen as a way to indicate progress and to raise any red flags that should be investigated. Decision making usually happens after the meeting, when something that needs action pops up.

Roadmaps and Sales Teams

It's impossible to talk about communication without mentioning roadmaps. Whenever I say "roadmap," product managers inherently cringe. Companies struggle with roadmaps because they've created Gantt charts in the past, and these charts basically say, "We're going to deliver this feature by January 18, and we're going to deliver this feature by March 20." A lot of roadmaps have been promised out to customers, and they're locked into place and can't be altered. This gets you into trouble when you realize you have overpromised and underdelivered.

Instead of thinking of roadmaps as a Gantt chart, you should view them as an explanation of strategy and the current stage of your product. This combines the strategic goals with the themes of work and the emerging product deliverables from it. To do this, the product roadmap should be updated constantly, especially at the team levels. This is why, at Produx Labs, we call them *Living Roadmaps*.

Roadmaps are not one-size-fits-all. You need to communicate them differently, depending on whether you are talking internally to your team about uncertainty or to the sales team about features that it can communicate to customers. You should design your communication to match your audience.

One great resource for determining how to set a roadmap is C. Todd Lombardo and Bruce McCarthy's book, *Product Roadmaps Relaunched*. It's an in-depth, practical guide on how to create great roadmaps for your company.

Usually, our roadmaps consist of a few key parts:

- The theme
- Hypothesis
- Goals and success metrics
- Stage of development
- Any important milestones

I recommend aligning your company around certain terminology to determine stages of development so everyone understands which activities are happening. We use these four phases:

Experiment

> This phase is to understand the problem and to determine whether it's worth solving. Teams in this phase are conducting problem exploration and solution exploration activities. No production code is being created.

Alpha

> This phase is to determine whether the solution is desirable to the customers. This is a minimum feature set or a robust solution experiment, but built in production code and live for a small set of users. These users understand that they are getting early access to a feature that might change or be killed, if it is not solving their problems.

Beta

> This phase is to determine whether the solution is scalable, from a technical standpoint. Although not always needed, this is a good phase to reduce risk. This release is available to more customers than the Alpha phase, but is still only a smaller subset of the entire population, since we are still testing. At this point, we've proven that the solution is desirable to customers, so it is unlikely that this feature will be killed unless it is not technically stable.

Generally Available (GA)

> This phase means that the solution is widely available to all of our clients. Sales teams can talk openly about GA products and can sell as much as possible to the target market.

Not only does aligning around terminology help communication with leaders, but it also assists with other parts of the business. Poorly-constructed roadmaps are the source of much tension between product and sales. If I had a nickel for every time a product manager told me that they hate their sales team, I wouldn't have to write this book—I would have bought an island somewhere in the South Pacific, where I could drink out of a coconut all day. But, alas, complaints are not real currency.

Although communicating status can be scary, given the variable nature of software development, it's also necessary. Product management enables the sales strategy. As I mentioned in the first section of the book, it's dangerous to be a sales-led organization because it can lead to a lack of alignment around strategy. But sales still needs something to sell. Creating working agreements and road-maps that can be communicated to customers is key to developing a good relationship between product and sales. You can make an agreement with the sales team that anything being released as GA—or anything further along in Beta—can be added to its sales roadmap.

Great communication, in the form of working agreements, meeting cadences, and roadmaps, can solve many of the alignment problems in the company. It can especially help move a company from being sales-led to product-led. But it takes a lot of work to put all of this together. This is why you need a product operations team.

Product Operations

When companies consist of just a handful of product teams, it is fairly easy to keep track of what's going on. Leaders can walk over to the product managers to learn about progress on goals. Processes are usually determined at the team level. Coordination is not a large concern.

But, as product teams scale to more than a few teams, keeping track of progress, goals, and processes becomes a challenge. This was the frustration Chris was explaining about not being able to see progress. Deploying the strategy and goals, understanding success of experimentation, and reporting on progress was too much work for the product leaders of Marquetly alone. They needed to focus on growing their product, and operations work was getting to be too much of a distraction.

To help distribute the work, we ended up implementing a product operations team, run by a chief of staff who reported to the CPO. The chief of staff created a very small team (two people) to help her streamline operations and reporting. They oversaw the cadences of strategy, found an analytics partner to set up tracking, and collected and organized the progress toward goals into reports for executives. This allowed the product people to focus on what they were good at, while product operations helped them to make informed decisions, by surfacing up those reports.

In larger organizations, you need the same thing, but at scale. We call this team *product operations*. In growth stage companies, a chief of staff (under the CPO, like in Marquetly), runs it. In larger organizations, the product operations team still reports to the CPO but it needs an experienced leader, usually at the VP level, to oversee it. This team is in charge of streamlining all operational and process work that product teams need to be successful. This includes:

- Create automated and streamlined ways to collect data on progress toward goals and outcomes across teams.
- Report on goals, outcomes, roadmaps, progress, capacity, and costs across the product organization, translating these activities into financial implications for the company executives.
- Set up and maintain a product analytics platform to report on product engagement metrics across the organization.
- Standardize product processes that go across teams, such as strategy cadences, experimentation tracking and feedback, documentation on product features, collecting data, setting goals, creating and maintaining roadmaps, and sales enablement.
- Organize and run critical product meetings for strategy creation, strategy deployment, and releases.
- Conduct any coaching or training for the product teams.

The point of this team is not to dictate how the members of a team work together to build the product but, instead, to create the criteria for inputs and outputs of the work. For example, they are not creating the product roadmap for the teams. They are creating a system and template for teams to input their goals, themes, progress, and details that can then be shared around the organization. They are not dictating whether a team can talk to users. They are creating systems that help teams figure out which users to target for their experimentation.

The product operations team should be made up of a combination of project managers and product people. It's good to allocate a few developers to this team, as well, so they can integrate with third parties, if needed, or build custom tools to fit a specific purpose.

We implemented a product operations team at a company I worked with that had over 350 Scrum teams. Up until then, they had no standardization around releasing or testing, let alone surfacing up goals. The CPO was frustrated, feeling paralyzed to make decisions about the portfolio without the right information.

When we spun up the team, I told the new VP of product operations, "Success for you would be automating away your team." As a product manager, she understood. This is not a team that is meant to be large. It's an efficiency engine dedicated to automating, streamlining, and optimizing. Although the team will probably never go away, since there is so much work to be done in this area, it should never strive to be larger than it needs to be.

A product operations team is a critical component to a well-run product organization at scale. It promotes good communication and alignment of the organization. But these things alone do not automatically produce a product mindset throughout the company. Reporting on outcomes can start to change behavior, but frequently, I've seen companies get this far and hit a wall. That's because they often change their processes, while continuing to reward people for the old ways of working.

21

Rewards and Incentives

Rewards and incentives are motivators for the employees of every company. The biggest issue I see with companies trying to transition to becoming product-led is that they don't evaluate their current reward structures to make sure they incentivize the right behavior.

I worked with a company in which everyone's bonuses were paid out based on a corporate scorecard. Every year, the company would go into yearly planning, determine what it wanted to accomplish, add it to the scorecard, and assign people to it. Much of the scorecard was made up of items to deliver, rather than goals to hit.

When I was first interviewing the product leaders about how they were measured for success, they all laughed. "Do you want to know what we do in December? We stop everything we're doing and look at the scorecard. If we haven't delivered on the items there, because they were really not as important as we thought a year ago, we just start building anything that will satisfy those requirements. Melissa, we literally ship whatever shit we can build in time that will check that box. Come January, we spend all our time pulling apart all the sloppy code. But, hey, we all get our bonuses in March."

Basically, everyone was wasting a month out of the year just trying to meet these goals so that they could get their bonuses, which represented a significant part of their salaries. Disaster.

It would shock you the number of times I've heard product managers say, "It doesn't matter what the goal is. We just have to deliver this feature." These are *good* product managers, too. They want to build great products—they just don't believe they can do so in their current environment. They are being forced into the build trap by company policy, even when they know it's the wrong way to build things.

Tying livelihoods to the fact that you shipped product at all, instead of learning or solving problems for customers, is what gets people into the build trap. It also means that people are afraid to try anything new. This mentality stifles innovation. Even though many people are seeking training and would like to work with good product management principles, they are afraid that doing so will prevent them from making money. If we are holding people accountable to new ways of working in these large company transformations, why are we judging their success with outdated methods?

Although it's easy to think that much of this is out of a product manager's control, given that the C-Suite and leaders of an organization usually set the rules for incentives, that might not be the complete truth. My advice for people is to push back. I know it's scary, but it can also be effective. I once had a product manager attend one of my workshops at a conference. At the end, she came up and told me that she thinks she is building the wrong thing: "I want to talk to my boss about it, but I'm afraid. I'm basically putting myself out of a job because I'm saying the product I own is not the right product to build. My entire bonus is tied to launching this thing."

We talked through an action plan for her organizational policies, and she went back and presented her case to her boss. She explained that she had analyzed the strategy for the division, and she had preliminary data that suggested that the product they were building was not a good idea. Her boss listened, and he agreed with her. They worked out how to sunset the product over two months. He ended up moving her to a more important product and gave her more seniority on the team—a win-win situation.

Even though it's difficult to change many of the policies, if you don't have the seniority, you can still try to change the minds of the people who can bring those messages up the chain. This can start the right dialogue. Talk to your bosses about what success really means. Define your metrics for when you know you will be done. Use this framework to spark the conversation in your reviews. And always come with data.

Rewards and incentives don't just affect the actions of product teams, but they also affect other parts of the organization. A notable department is sales. Most sales teams are held accountable to selling—signing the contracts and bringing in the revenue. Many teams overpromise in order to make their commission numbers, which are usually large parts of their salaries.

I've worked on teams that had a sales department which oversold the road-maps so much that we were two years behind in development. Customers were angry, and we had high churn. I also saw sales teams target the wrong customers in order to make numbers. These customers left quickly. We still want to incentivize sales teams to keep selling, but adjusting the components of their salary so that their livelihood does not depend too much on commission percentages can help to mitigate this risk. Tying retention numbers to their success metrics can also help to ensure that they target the right people.

If you are a leader at a company, it's time to reevaluate how you are incentivizing people. You should be rewarding people for moving the business forward—achieving outcomes, learning about your users, and finding the right business opportunities. At the end of the day, the rest is just vanity metrics.

22

Safety and Learning

In addition to reward structures that prevent people from innovating, the culture of the organization plays a big part. You might not be judging your teams for success based only on outputs, but they may still not be willing to try new things. Why? There may not be enough safety in the organization to fail and learn.

Marquetly was successful because the CEO and leaders held back while the teams were experimenting, even if that made them squirm a bit. Product managers need a certain amount of trust from the organization to have room to explore different options. To really push boundaries, teams are going to have to try some perceivably wild stuff. It might not be the solution you originally thought of and the teams might not have all the answers at the beginning, but if they are not allowed to explore these weird paths, they will never push the status quo. The status quo is safe. The status quo keeps you from innovating.

This doesn't mean that we should be failing in spectacular ways. With the rise of Lean Startup, we began to focus on outcomes, yes, but we also started to celebrate failure. I want to be clear here: it is not a success if you fail and do not learn. Learning should be at the core of every product-led organization. It should be what drives us as an organization.

It is just better to fail in smaller ways, earlier, and to learn what will succeed, rather than spending all the time and money failing in a publicly large way. This is why we have problem and solution exploration in product management—to de-risk failing in the market.

Now, sometimes, we fail in the most spectacular way possible. How we respond to these situations really determines our company culture. I love the story of Netflix trying to break into two companies. Netflix tried to split off its DVD business in 2011 as Qwikster. It was a complete disaster in the market. People were very angry, canceling their subscriptions and writing scathing articles.

Many articles bashed Netflix, saying this fiasco would be the end of the company. Netflix responded, quickly rolling back the change.

This was a failure that many people thought Netflix couldn't come back from, but look at the company now. The CEO apologized, explained that the choices it made were not core to its strategy, and stated that it was going to get back to its roots in satisfying customers through exceptional on-demand entertainment. The company picked itself back up and went along. And it never used that experience to stifle innovation. Fast-forward a few years, and Netflix was creating their own TV shows, a huge experiment. This message was loud and clear —Netflix is a safe, innovative place that pushes the boundaries.

Many companies talk about how they want their people to be innovative and how they want to create crazy new products, but there has to be an understanding that it's safe to fail in order to get innovation. When you don't have safety built in to your company, your product managers won't feel comfortable trying something new. No one will.

Corporations love to talk about risk management. The irony is that experimentation is the ultimate risk-management strategy because, when you experiment early, you can prevent the failure of something you will have spent billions of dollars on later. Netflix could have tested the waters with Qwikster. Instead, it went full force on an idea that hadn't been validated. The company was fortunate enough to be able to get immediate feedback and to change course, but that's not always the case for companies.

So many companies fail slowly. They release products and never measure whether those products do anything. They just let them sit there, collecting dust in a sea of endless features, never knowing whether they are producing value. This is the more dangerous and costly way to fail. Taking 10 years to fail, slowly burning through cash and never getting anywhere, is more problematic than allowing for smaller failures along the way.

Instead, if you adopt a great product mindset and you give people the freedom to fail, what you're doing is allowing them to fail quickly, quietly, and at a lower cost because they're testing things early. That's the type of failure you want to encourage. That's the type of failure from which we can recover.

Ideally, product managers should be risk mitigators who say, "Hey, I think the most costly thing we can do is build this product without knowing it's the right product to build. How do I test it and ensure that this is actually what we want? How do I become more confident that we're on the right path before I invest money in this?" Leaders who give people the room to do that see the best results and avoid the build trap.

It's also the leader's job to give people boundaries within which to operate. Leaders can say, "Okay, you're going to go experiment, but you can only spend $100,000 on this experiment. We don't want to invest more. Come back to us when you know what's going on, and then we'll be able to think about investing more money."

There are many different ways to create boundaries. One way I frequently recommend is to segment your user base into populations for Alpha and Beta testing, like I mentioned in the communication chapter. That means, instead of launching the product to everyone, start with a small representative population, learn from them, and then expand to more people as you feel more confident. This approach cuts down on the publicity needed for a proper launch and lets you contain the rollback, if the product doesn't work.

The first experiment is always the scariest, for everyone—leaders and product managers. I advise product managers to have the boundaries conversation to make it less scary. Explain to your boss the possible impact of your experiments. How are you going to mitigate risk? How can you save money?

The first experiment I ever ran was at the celebrity e-commerce company that I talked about earlier. The CEO had a great idea to get our celebrity sellers' personalities into the marketing of our products. The execution was still up for debate. The first idea was to apply a Twitter-like interface to our home page, meaning that the celebrities could post messages about whatever they liked there. I decided to run an experiment to see whether it would help increase sales.

We spent two days building a simple way to test whether messages were effective on those pages. We tested the feature with a small subset of users— enough to generate real data. At the end of the week, we found that we did not increase sales at all. We pivoted and tried a different approach using emails to communicate with the fans. That increased sales by three times! I calculated out how much fully executing on the original idea would have cost and compared it to the cost of the second idea. I went back to the CEO and explained, "We just saved $250,000 and increased our sales three times by this other way of working." He was ecstatic! We not only saved a ton of money, we hit our goals many times over.

By demonstrating, in small ways, the importance of this style of working, I was able to gain the buy-in from my organization and get the safety I needed. Not all of my experiments were hits, but by communicating how the approach helped us de-risk the solution that we eventually chose, my organization trusted me to keep going.

If you are a product manager, think about how you can change your message to your boss and begin to gain trust by working this way. If you are a manager, be open to the possibility that new ways of working are also beneficial and be ready to help your product manager establish boundaries, rather than saying no to them. And, finally, if you are an executive, think about how you can create safe spaces for people to learn.

23

Budgeting

One of the factors that leads to the output-over-outcome mindset in organizations is the way that they do budgeting. A CTO of a global financial services company once asked me for advice. As he moved up through the ranks in the organization, he realized that many of the issues it faced were a result of the way it was budgeting.

He explained it to me, "Every year, we go into a yearly planning cycle. The management of the organization asks all the VPs what they plan to deliver. They have the product managers write business cases, which they choose to fund. Those business cases are based off very little data, and they have some wild estimates on them. They turn all these business cases into a giant roadmap for the year, give them out to each team, and fund the projects. At the end of the year, if they do not deliver what's on the roadmap, they do not get as much funding the next year."

"Do you realize what that means, Melissa?" he asked me. "That means that, if a team finds a way to build a product cheaper—or finds that the product shouldn't be built at all—they are building it anyway because they will be penalized if they don't spend all their money."

That. Is. Insane. Because these budgets are done on a yearly basis, it also really kills the team's ability to change course at all throughout the year. The organization is preventing itself from rapidly learning and iterating.

It's far wiser to look at funding product development like a venture capitalist (VC). Startups must pitch investors on their vision and on the data they collect to prove that the vision will be viable and profitable in the market. They go to VCs and say, "This is where we are. These are our next goals. We need this much money to get to those goals." The investment that VCs give the companies helps them get to the next level, until they are profitable. But, if, for whatever reason, the company can't get to the next level, the funding stops and ends up allocated to another company that can get the VC a return on its investment.

Product-led companies invest in and budget for work based on their portfolio distribution and the stage of their work. This means allocating the appropriate funds across product lines for things that are *known knowns* and ready to be built, and it means setting aside money to invest in discovering new opportunities that will propel your business model forward. They then allocate more and more funds to grow the opportunities as they become validated.

So, for example, if a team is trying to build out a new product line as a way of generating a new revenue stream for the business, it might ask for $50,000 to get started and explore this new area to see whether they're on to something. After they've proven that there is a market and have shown the data that it will succeed, the team could ask for $250,000 to do more exploration or to begin product development. They explore, they understand, they figure out what's working, and, over the next six months, they might build a small-scale version to start putting in front of users. If people adopt the product, the team can go back and ask for a much larger amount, in the millions, to scale and fund its efforts to grow the product line.

This was the biggest shift for Marquetly. The company had to break out of its old way of budgeting once a year. Instead, it allocated funds to the product portfolio as a whole. Then it used the product initiative reviews to determine what should be funded, based on the amount of certainty toward the outcomes.

Not all investments start off tiny. Depending on the opportunity and how much data you have, you might initially want to fuel it with more funds. But the idea is that all budgeting should be tied to getting a product to the next stage. It's an effective way to both focus the teams and make sure you're not overspending.

24

Customer Centricity

Having the right communication, rewards, incentives, budgeting, policies, and safety are all important in an organization, but one more thing is still required to make you truly product-led. In addition to a culture that rewards and promotes learning, you need a culture that focuses on the customer. Many of the top companies today, such as Amazon, Netflix, Zappos, Dollar Shave Club, and Disney, have gotten where they are by focusing on the customer. You can see this attitude manifest in the way that executives talk about and treat their customers.

One of the most famous Jeff Bezos quotes about how Amazon succeeds is, "The most important single thing is to focus obsessively on the customer. Our goal is to be earth's most customer-centric company." This approach really defines everything that Amazon does, and it pays off. It grew its Prime membership from 25 million in 2012 to more than 100 million in 2018, by making it easier for people to shop and find what they need on Amazon, with free two-day shipping and access to lots of entertainment.

This is the core of what it means to be customer-centric—to put yourself into your customers' shoes and ask, "What would make my customers happy and move our business forward?" In the beginning of this book, we talked about product management being a value exchange. Being customer-centric allows you to figure out what products and services will fulfill that value on the customer side.

Another company that understands the importance of being customer-centric is John Deere, a farming technology company located in Iowa. When I interviewed one of its product managers, Kevin Seidl, he explained to me that John Deere encouraged his team to actively go see its customers in action. "They knew that, if they were hiring software engineers, we weren't experts in farming. All the developers are from urban areas and have no idea that there's a difference in the types of corn you would grow. So they encourage us to go out and see our farmers work in real life."

John Deere sends its people to a fully-functioning farm set up a few miles from the office. It's a real, running farm with equipment that people can come try out before deciding to buy. The engineers and product managers all go out there, too, to learn more about farming. John Deere also has people in the organization who are farmers for fun. Many of the software teams spend Fridays helping them turn over their crops.

However, the true mark of John Deere's commitment to this way of working is seen when times get tough. Seidl explained that, even when economic times were tough for the company, he has always been allowed to visit his customers.

This is what it means to be customer centric: knowing that the most important thing you can do to create great products is to deeply understand your customers. This is also the core of what it means to be product-led.

You can focus on outcomes over outputs, have the right people in the right roles, follow the motions to create a good strategy deployment process, make sure you have the right structure and policies, and still not escape the build trap. That's because escaping it is not just about following the motions—it's about an entire organizational change.

25

Marquetly: The Product-Led Company

It took a few more years for Marquetly to completely escape the build trap. Many of its people had been working with an output mentality for a very long time. These people didn't initially believe in this new way of working, but, as full results began trickling in over the next few years, it was difficult to argue with the numbers. Marquetly was able to achieve its strategic intents, growing its revenue in the enterprise and individual markets, which resulted in it being acquired for a very large sum of money by a larger educational company.

The company continued to prioritize its strategy on a rolling basis until it reached its goals. The artificial time bounds of yearly budgeting and strategy creation disappeared. Instead, the company took an investment-minded approach, budgeting each year for growth strategies, while funding initiatives that the product teams validated through experimentation and research. Marquetly ended up killing a lot of its ideas early on. That allowed it to focus on what really mattered to achieve its goal.

Marquetly was successful because it had a leader who understood that change started with him. Chris knew that, if he did not adopt the outcome-oriented mindset, the customer centricity, and the comfort with uncertainty, no one else in his organization would. "How can I possibly expect the rest of my organization to change, if I am not willing to?" he told me early on.

Even though it was difficult for him to adapt at first, he persevered because he believed in what being product led would achieve. One of the biggest mistakes that companies make in these transitions is having leadership think that it's everyone else's job to change instead of theirs. I explained to Chris how I had seen some major transformations fail because they were delegated. He listened.

He surrounded himself with smart product leaders, like CPO Jen, and then trusted his team to achieve the outcomes. They brought in more senior product people to train the junior product people. Christa and her team became an early success story, shared through the organization and recounted to new hires so that they would understand they could think outside the box.

Christa rose through the ranks of Marquetly rather quickly. When the company was acquired, she ended up being promoted to the VP of product in charge of exploring new business lines at the larger educational company. Bringing her experimental mindset to a much larger company was not easy, but with the seniority came more opportunity and authority to change how people perceived building products.

The Marquetly team was able to escape the build trap by implementing a customer-centric product management division, supporting them with the right strategy and then enabling their processes of experimentation with safety and policies that promoted learning. By focusing on the outcomes instead of on the outputs, it was able to actually achieve them.

Getting out of the build trap is possible, but it takes time and effort. It's not something that you can easily achieve in a year. It requires not only changing how you work but also how you think as an organization. It needs the participation of everyone in the organization, from the leaders in the C-Suite to the product managers on the teams. Reading this book is your first step. Setting up a fully-functioning product organization will be your first leap.

Afterword: Escaping the Build Trap to Become Product-Led

Someone recently asked me, "What is the most important thing you learned through your career as a product manager?"

I was a bit stumped. See, there wasn't just one thing I had learned—but many things I needed to learn at different stages of my career.

When I was first starting off as a product manager, I needed to learn about humility. I learned that my role was not that of the big idea generator but that of the bad idea terminator. I needed to learn to be humble and to gain the support and buy-in of my team in order to make great products. Experimenting with my team taught me the power of data. Data beats any opinion every time.

As I moved on to more senior roles, I learned that having a good strategic framework could make or break a company. That if you did not judge people for success by outcomes, you would never achieve those outcomes. I watched a few companies crumble under the weight of a bad strategic framework.

Becoming a consultant taught me about the power of personalities in an organization. People will get in the way of a good product every time. Even if it is the best idea for the company, if it doesn't meet the personal agendas of senior stakeholders, it can be squashed. To mitigate that risk, you need to deeply understand what motivates people and to know how you can address their personal motivations by introducing information and data that wins them over.

Consulting also taught me that one of the quickest ways to kill the spirit of a great employee is to put them in an environment where they can't succeed. That's when most people leave. Even good product managers become tired of waking up and going to war every day. They spend too much time trying to change the policies so that they can succeed at their job rather than building the best product they can.

The truth is that most organizations out there are not product-led. And yet, being product-led is a winning strategy. If you look at some of the best companies out there today—Amazon, Netflix, and Google, for example—they are not reactively building whatever customer request comes their way. They are not following Agile processes blindly to build whatever features they can, as fast as they can. Instead, they are developing products with the intent to deliver value to their customers.

Being agile, being customer-centric—these things are already baked into their culture. They understand that the fundamental criterion for building a product is that the product solves a problem for a user. They do not just build things for the sake of checking boxes. They build things to further their business.

Ten years ago, when I started my journey in product management, I looked around and could barely find any peers. Now, smart and talented product managers abound, looking for the right organizations. They want to join product-led organizations, and they want to build kick-ass products that their customers love. It is my hope that more organizations will escape the build trap, empower these product managers to thrive, and create products that we all enjoy.

So, if you want to determine whether yours is a product-led company—or how far you might be from one—I leave you with these final six questions, which are the ones I ask whenever I am brought in to evaluate whether a company has escaped the build trap. They are also the questions that I suggest product managers ask during their interviews to see whether this will be the right environment in which for them to operate.

How do you stack up to being product-led?

Appendix: Six Questions to Determine Whether a Company Is Product-Led

Who came up with the last feature or product idea you built?

If I ask a product manager this question, I hope to see a look of confusion on his or her face. "What do you mean who came up with it? Well, our team did. Right? That's how it normally works." This kind of response is a sign of a healthy product management organization, in which management sets the goals and the team is given room to figure out how to reach them. The product manager should be leading the charge to discover user problems and to solve them. This doesn't mean that an important initiative or solution idea can't come from management every once in a while, but that should be the exception, not the rule.

It's a huge red flag when a team not only can't take ownership for what it is building, but can't even tell me *why* it is building it. This means that the originator of the idea never connected the *why* to the *what*.

What was the last product you decided to kill?

Another sign of an unhealthy product management culture is the inability to kill a product or idea that will not help a company reach its goals. If you hear, "We never really kill anything," it often means that there's a pretty big problem.

Typically, this happens for one of the following reasons:

- *The organization already committed the idea to customers.* Often, some-one from marketing has promised a client that a particular feature is in the works and then the company feels committed to fully follow through with it. It doesn't matter whether the client actually requested it or whether it achieves any of the organization's desired goals.
- *Budgeting can't budge.* In some large organizations, in which the budget is set at the beginning of the year, the team must spend all of it or else it will not receive an equally large budget the following year. This concept is baffling, but it happens.
- *No pushback to management.* Again, a lack of testing and questioning potential features signifies a lack of empowerment in a team. If a team doesn't feel like it is safe to say to management, "Hey, that thing we tested, well, it doesn't work and we don't think it's worth the money to build it," the chances of a successful environment for product management are slim.

When's the last time you talked with your customers?

What I dread hearing is, "Oh, well, management doesn't really let us talk to customers. They're worried about us annoying them too much."

Without a healthy dialogue between a company and its customers, there is no way to truly learn about what the customers want or need. An organization set up for success not only allows product managers to talk to customers, it encourages them to do so and recognizes this process as a huge part of the job. In fact, your interviewee should be probing *you* for clues that you are comfortable talking to customers and that you aren't planning to spend all your time safely indoors writing user stories.

What is your goal?

This is the first question I ask any product manager during an interview process.[1] If the product manager cannot articulate a clear goal, it's a sign of poor product management at the organizational level. If the product manager does have a goal but it is more output centric than outcome focused, this also signifies an unhealthy product team. An output-centric team measures success in terms of meeting product shipment deadlines. It pays little attention to what these products are actually doing for its business.

---

1 "Interviewing for the Job is Product Management," *http://bit.ly/2JgKR9X*.

The purpose of a product manager is to create value for the business by creating value for the customer. If the product manager does not understand the vision of the company, how are they supposed to figure out how to get there? Goals should be outcome oriented, actionable, and clearly communicated throughout the organization.

What are you currently working on?

A truly successful product manager talks more passionately about the problems the product development team is solving than the solutions they are shipping. This is one of the biggest signs of success, for me, and it goes hand-in-hand with the question of goals. When I ask product managers this question, I want to hear about what big problems they are tackling for the user and the business. Of course, they will talk about the solution, as well, but more in the context of what it will do to help solve their problems. If this mindset is encouraged throughout the organization, you can hear it echoed at all levels.

What are your product managers like?

As product managers, we want to work in an organization where the role is respected and well regarded. I've seen many organizations where the product management function was not well-respected. There were two causes: product managers were either seen as too strong, or they were seen as too weak.

In the first instance, product managers were seen as dictators who threw out requirements to the team rather than involving them in their decision-making process. The teams grew resentful and felt they were treated as resources rather than as colleagues. A good product manager knows that getting buy-in from the whole team is crucial. The product manager is not the only person who should be coming up with the ideas but should instead be harnessing their team's full capacity. A sign of a healthy product team is hearing development and UX people say, "I love my product manager. She has clear direction, communicates well, and helps keep us stay focused on the goals and problems."

In the second instance, product managers are seen as weak in the organization because they are beaten down by stakeholders[2] and management. When product managers are seen as project managers, they hold no

---

2 "Rallying Stakeholders is Product Management," *http://bit.ly/2z9QIhQ.*

decision-making power. Stakeholders and management use them to just usher their own ideas through. Product managers don't feel like they can say no because of the potential for strong backlash.

The dream organization for product people is one that sees product managers as leaders who help shape the direction of the company and the services they provide to their customers. They are respected as partners in steering the ship forward. These six questions can help you to ensure that the company you are in—or want to join—will support and encourage you to do everything you can to succeed.

Index

Symbols

About the Author

Melissa Perri believes the key to creating great products is growing great product leaders. As the CEO of Produx Labs, she helps companies effectively scale their product organizations. Melissa also founded the online school Product Institute, and started a program to train the next generation of chief product officers. She is an internationally recognized, sought-after keynote speaker. Melissa graduated from Cornell University with a B.S. in operations research and information engineering.